D1210325

WHAT ARE THEY SAYING ABOUT
NEW TESTAMENT APOCALYPTIC?

What Are They Saying About New Testament Apocalyptic?

Scott M. Lewis, S.J.

PAULIST PRESS
New York/Mahwah, N.J.

Cover design by Jim Brisson

Book design by Theresa Sparacio

Copyright © 2004 by Scott M. Lewis

All rights reserved. No part of this book may be reproduced or transmitted in any form or by any means, electronic or mechanical, including photocopying, recording, or by any information storage and retrieval system without permission in writing from the Publisher.

Library of Congress Cataloging-in-Publication Data

Lewis, Scott M., 1948–
   What are they saying about New Testament apocalyptic? / Scott M. Lewis.
      p.   cm.
   Includes bibliographical references.
   ISBN 0-8091-4228-7 (alk. paper)
   1. Apocalyptic literature—History and criticism. 2. Bible. N.T.—Criticism, interpretation, etc. 3. Eschatology—Biblical teaching. I. Title.

BS646.L49 2003
225′.046—dc22

                                                                2003022455

Published by Paulist Press
997 Macarthur Boulevard
Mahwah, New Jersey 07430

www.paulistpress.com

Printed and bound in the
United States of America

Contents

Acknowledgments

I am grateful to Regis College, Toronto, for granting me a one-semester leave for the preparation of this book. The use of the fine library at St. Paul's University, Ottawa, and the assistance of its helpful staff made my work much easier. My thanks also to the Jesuit community in Ottawa.

In the spring of 1999, I offered a course on apocalyptic in the New Testament. It was made most enjoyable by the active participation and creativity of the students.

Conversations with friends and their encouragement were most important to me. In this regard, I would like to express my gratitude to Ron Mercier, S.J., Rob Allore, S.J., Ms. Heather Gamester, Cathleen Flynn, C.S.J., Rosemary MacDonald, C.S.M., Michael Stoeber, Frank and Anne Jankulak, Susan Severino, and Annie Straussberg Tung.

A special thanks to Rosemary MacDonald and Kay Lewis for a careful proofreading of the text and for their comments. I dedicate the book to my parents, Ray and Kay Lewis, with love.

Introduction:
The End Is Near!

> *But in those days, after that suffering, the sun will be dark-*
> *ened, and the moon will not give its light, and the stars will*
> *be falling from heaven, and the powers in the heavens will*
> *be shaken. Then they will see 'the Son of Man coming in*
> *clouds' with great power and glory. Then he will send out*
> *the angels, and gather his elect from the four winds, from*
> *the ends of the earth to the ends of heaven.* (Mark 13:24–27)

This vivid and evocative description of the last days and the return of the Lord seems to match the image that many people have of apocalyptic literature. Indeed, the word *apocalyptic* has entered our vocabulary to describe chaos, destruction, cataclysm, and the end of the world.

The recent passage to the new millennium has kindled a renewed interest in New Testament (NT) passages of this type, for they have become objects of increased interest and speculation in many churches and in elements of secular society. For some people, 2000 is merely another date on the calendar. For others, it is the countdown to Armageddon. In many cities, zealous individuals distribute leaflets on street corners warning of impending cosmic disaster. Others warn of the Beast of Revelation—the Antichrist—who seeks to enslave humanity with his latest instruments of choice, the cash register bar code and implanted microchips. The "Left Behind" novels, based on the Book of Revelation, enjoy immense popularity.

1

Even a secular apocalyptic event such as the Y2K bug was coopted by Christian apocalyptic speculation. In some millenarian churches the date for the end of the world has been set and reset, causing many to sell all of their property and await the coming of the Lord. There are tragic elements in this frenzy, as the events of Waco and the New Age suicide cults demonstrate so well. From many pulpits and television channels, the message is the same: The predictions contained in the book of Revelation are about to be fulfilled, and one should be spiritually prepared.

These spiritual exhortations and predictions of the end all base their proclamation on the apocalyptic passages contained in the New Testament, particularly in the Book of Revelation. These portions of the Bible have provided the fuel for millenarian speculation and end-time sects for the last two thousand years, and they promise to do so for some time to come.

How are we to interpret them in a manner that will respect both the sanctity of the text, the results of biblical scholarship, and the needs of believers in our own times? Frankly, the apocalyptic portions of the New Testament perplex and embarrass us. Seldom, if ever, do we hear a homily based upon these themes. We don't really understand them. What are we to do with the Book of Revelation and those parts of the New Testament that predict an imminent end of the world? How do we interpret the cosmology that we might not share? As one writer stated so well, we are baffled by pages that contain

> a weird and wonderful world of fantasy and dreams—beasts with sprouting horns, dragons spouting fire, falling stars, mysterious horsemen, mystical mountains, sacred rivers, devastating earthquakes, fearsome giants, demon progeny, monstrous births, portents in heaven and portents on earth. Its often frenzied and frenetic descriptions of coming woes sound like the product of overheated minds.[1]

Faced with the dissonance of cataclysmic symbolism on the one hand and the progression of mundane events and the demands of everyday life on the other, we prefer to ignore them and pass on some of the more consoling and edifying passages we find in the Gospels and the letters of St. Paul.

But there is another often ignored aspect of apocalyptic literature that heralds a message of hope and newness. The image of the New Jerusalem is one with which most of us are familiar:

> Then I saw a new heaven and a new earth; for the first heaven and the first earth had passed away, and the sea was no more. And I saw the holy city, the new Jerusalem, coming down out of heaven from God, prepared as a bride adorned for her husband. And I heard a loud voice from the throne saying, "See, the home of God is among mortals. He will dwell with them…; they will be his peoples, and God himself will be with them; he will wipe every tear from their eyes. Death will be no more; mourning and crying and pain will be no more, for the first things have passed away." And the one who was seated on the throne said, "See, I am making all things new." (Rev 21:1–6)

This beautiful passage has been a source of comfort to many, especially in the context of a funeral liturgy. We believe it speaks to us of the beauty and peace of heaven. It might surprise us to know that this is a passage from an apocalypse that describes God's action in history, on earth, and not in the hereafter. We begin to see that perhaps there is much about the apocalyptic message that we do not adequately understand.

J. Christiaan Beker claims that a refusal to take apocalyptic theology seriously encourages false apocalyptic movements—which he calls "neo-apocalypticism"—to flourish. These false interpretations are based on two mistaken assumptions. The first is the predictability of future events as prophesied by an infallible scripture; and second, divine determinism and control of all events leading up to the end of history. They also claim to be able to correlate the symbolism and prophecies of the Bible with current events, leaving one with the conclusion that all history has been leading up to and focused on the time in which one lives. This, says Beker, is narcissistic, nonparticipatory, self-centered, and lacking a theology of the cross.[2] Wise words, but the "mistaken assumptions" have long lives and show no signs of running out of steam.

There are many competing interpretations of these apocalyptic passages of the New Testament. The pressures and uncertainties of the new millennium underscore the need for a clearer understanding of the meaning and intent of apocalyptic literature in the New Testament and an appreciation of its contemporary value for the church. In the last thirty years there has been an effort to understand apocalyptic on its own terms and to reach a deeper appreciation of its purpose and function. Rather than being retrograde or outmoded, there is much in the apocalyptic message that speaks to our own human experience. Rather than being a script for the end of the world, apocalyptic literature and eschatology demonstrate how the divine and the human interact in the world, and the wonderful possibilities offered when humanity follows God's ways, as well as the disastrous consequences of the way opposed to God, that is, selfishness, greed, injustice, and oppression. It is meant to keep the flame of hope burning in the human heart with its persistent message that our struggle in this world has cosmic meaning.

A lack of precision and clarity regarding terms was (and still is in some cases) the cause of much confusion in scholarship. Terms are often used carelessly and interchangeably. In an attempt to be clearer and more precise about what is being discussed, many contemporary scholars make the following distinctions, which I will use in this book: "apocalypse" defines a particular literary genre; "apocalyptic eschatology" is a particular religious perspective and thought structure that may or may not be expressed in the form of an apocalypse; "apocalypticism" is a sociological ideology reflecting views found in an apocalyptic eschatology. These are closely related to one another, but do not always coincide exactly. For example, a particular work might contain apocalyptic eschatology, but might not be formally an apocalypse.

Many scholars have contributed to the search for a rigorous definition of apocalyptic literature and theology. We will survey the works of the principal scholars, such as Albert Schweitzer, H. Rowley, D. S. Russell, Ernst Käsemann, Klaus Koch, John Collins, Paul Hanson, J. Christiaan Beker, Adela Yarbro Collins, N. T. Wright, and Elisabeth. Schüssler-Fiorenza.

The question of apocalyptic elements in the New Testament must be considered in the context of contemporary historical Jesus research. Did Jesus actually utter the apocalyptic pronouncements found in the Gospels? Or were these the products of the early Christian movement? Here we enter the controversial and sometimes acrimonious historical Jesus debate. Dominic Crossan, Marcus Borg, and the Jesus Seminar have challenged the reigning view that the sayings and teachings of Jesus were apocalyptic in nature and that Jesus himself expected to see the end, which he prophesied in passages such as Mark 13. Utilizing a different methodology and additional sources, they believe that the earliest layers of the Jesus tradition are free of apocalyptic and that the Jesus they reconstruct from this research is someone who was primarily an itinerant teacher of subversive wisdom and/or a revolutionary social reformer.

But N. T. Wright, E. P. Sanders, Dale Allison, Paula Fredriksen, and Bart Ehrman, among others, have vigorously defended in one form or another the traditional view: Jesus was an apocalyptic prophet; many of the apocalyptic sayings attributed to him in fact were uttered by him, at least in some form; and he preached and expected the end within his lifetime, an end that did not come. Jesus is best understood within the framework of a first-century Jewish apocalyptic prophet.

We must return to Schweitzer again in analyzing the writings of Paul. His description of the apocalyptic nature of Paul's ministry, while being rightly challenged in many respects, is still important in the discussion. J. Beker continues in this approach as he seeks to reappropriate the apocalyptic nature and message of Paul's Gospel. Scholars such as Martinus de Boer, N. T. Wright, Elisabeth Schüssler-Fiorenza and others have elaborated on the import of this message.

Apocalyptic theology has often been accused of being otherworldly and contemptuous of human concerns. At its core, however, apocalyptic eschatology is a theology of hope in the face of persecution, oppression, and alienation. As such, it makes immediate and absolute demands on the individual: The world as we know it is transitory and ephemeral, the time is short, and one must begin living as if the renewed world has already been born.

Of special interest is the manner in which apocalyptic categories governed the spiritual and ethical life of the NT church. The apocalyptic elements in the New Testament raise issues such as salvation, sectarianism, and interreligious dialogue. Who is saved? Is there any other way except Christ? What about non-Christians? How do we preach and teach the apocalyptic elements of the New Testament in a way that gives life and hope, rather than stoking the fires of sectarianism, bigotry, and fear?

1
The Mother of All Theology

The word *apocalyptic* is often used to describe a catastrophic, chaotic event. The origin of the word is much simpler: It is a derivation of the Greek word *apokalypsis,* which means "revelation." The opening lines of the Book of Revelation read "the *apokalypsis* of Jesus Christ," and it is this book that has been so influential in defining both the genre apocalypse and much of the apocalyptic stream in Western consciousness. We use the term in a technical sense to describe a certain type of religious literature produced in a Jewish milieu during the period roughly 250 B.C.E. to 250 C.E. This includes both Jewish and Christian works, in addition to those that are confluences of both streams. Examples of apocalyptic works include 1 and 2 Enoch, Daniel, 4 Ezra, 2 and 3 Baruch, Apocalypse of Abraham, Testament of Levi 2—5, Apocalypse of Zephaniah, portions of Jubilees and the Testament of Abraham, and portions of the Old Testament (sometimes referred to as OT) such as Zechariah 9—14 and Isaiah 24—27. The Book of Revelation is the only representative of the genre apocalypse in the NT, but passages reflecting apocalyptic eschatology and imagery are found in the Gospels, nearly all the genuine letters of Paul, pseudo-Pauline works such as 2 Thessalonians, as well as letters such as Jude, James, and 1 and 2 Peter.

From the Enlightenment onward, apocalyptic fell from favor and began to be viewed with a negative and sometimes contemptuous eye. Koch states that in the last century, apocalyptic was in the opinion of many theologians the "quintessence of what is 'eschatologically' improper. Theological eschatology believed that it could best prove its legitimacy by abjuring apocalyptic as firmly and vocally as possible," an attitude that has lasted well into this century.[1]

Thoroughgoing Eschatology

Albert Schweitzer's *The Quest of the Historical Jesus,* in print nearly a century after its first publication, is still interesting, challenging, and entertaining to read. Schweitzer surveyed—mercilessly, but with great wit and insight—the attempts of eighteenth- and nineteenth-century scholarship to reconstruct the historical Jesus. He pointed out that most of the reconstructions bore eerie resemblances to their authors. It is his fundamental conclusion regarding the historical Jesus that interests us here: Building on the insights of Johannes Weiss, Schweitzer insisted that Jesus must be understood in the context of his own first-century Palestinian milieu, and that his ministry, mission, and teaching were products of his "thoroughgoing eschatology."[2]

According to Schweitzer, a Jewish eschatology that included both a cosmic Son of Man and necessary sufferings before the end was universally held, especially by Jesus. He expected the Son of Man to come before Jesus and his disciples completed their journey through the cities of Israel, and when that did not happen, he took it upon himself to suffer and force the arrival of the end (Mark 8:31–33).[3] In his vivid and evocative prose, Schweitzer describes the failed mission of Jesus:

> There is silence all around. The Baptist appears, and cries: "Repent, for the Kingdom of Heaven is at hand." Soon after that comes Jesus, and in the knowledge that He is the coming Son of Man lays hold of the wheel of the world to set it moving on that last revolution which is to bring all ordinary

The apocalypse as a literary form is characterized by: (a) discourse cycles, which can take the form of visions or auditions, between the recipient and heavenly counterpart; (b) spiritual turmoil, in which the recipient is often overcome by fright and dismay, sometimes falling to the ground or going into a trance; (c) moral exhortation discourses, in which an eschatological ethic unfolds; (d) pseudonymity, by which the author usually uses the name of a great biblical figure from the past; (e) mythical images rich in symbolism; (f) the composite nature of the texts.[18]

The term *apocalyptic* also describes certain "moods and ideas" present within a historical and intellectual movement, which can be found in many writings that might not be formally classified as belonging to the genre apocalypse. Apocalyptic is characterized by writings that are "dominated by an urgent expectation of the impending overthrow of all earthly conditions in the immediate future." This takes the form of a "vast cosmic catastrophe," and the end-time is closely connected with the previous history of humankind and of the cosmos. Time is divided into fixed segments, the contents of which have been predetermined from creation and encoded within portions of the prophetic books.[19]

The final redemption is accomplished by a "mediator with royal functions," described by various angelic, divine, or human terms. The term *glory* is used to describe the new age, especially the reconciliation and union of the earthly and heavenly spheres.[20]

Koch realizes that his motifs are distributed throughout various apocalypses, and that many of them can be found outside the genre. The key is the manner in which they are arranged, for apocalyptic events must be understood as the author's understanding of a definite sequence that runs "like a continuous scarlet thread running through the whole."[21]

Apocalyptic is "the revelation of a divine revelation," and in order to express this revelation in a coherent historical pattern rather than a linear logical one, a multiplicity of approaches is necessary. He insists that apocalyptic can be understood not only as a literary genre, but as an "expression of a particular attitude of mind." Koch's insights are useful in that they go beyond mere literary characteristics, and his work influenced Beker and others.[22]

Paul Hanson finds the genesis of apocalyptic in the crisis surrounding the "collapse of a well-ordered world view which defines values and orders the universe." Apocalyptic eschatology is a religious perspective focusing on privileged revelation to the elect of the "cosmic vision of Yahweh's sovereignty—especially as it relates to his acting to deliver his faithful...." Apocalyptic eschatology arose from the prophetic eschatology of the Old Testament. Alienation is elemental in the generation of apocalyptic, for pessimism has caused the visionaries to retreat from "plain history, real politics, and human instrumentality."[23]

In a later essay, Hanson distinguishes between the genre apocalypse: the perspective of apocalyptic eschatology, and apocalypticism as a religious movement. The first is very loosely defined as a medium for communicating the apocalyptic message, characterized by ecstasy and rapture, angelic guides, and encouragement to those undergoing persecution. The Book of Revelation is used as the paradigm. The second is a perspective that "views divine plans in relation to historical realities in a particular way." He views these distinctions as merely a useful heuristic tool and cautions against rigidity in their application.[24]

Apocalypticism is a socioreligious movement that is latent within apocalyptic eschatology, and its generation occurs at the "point where the disappointments of history lead a group to embrace that perspective as an ideology, using it moreover to resolve the contradictions between traditional hopes and frustrating historical realities...."[25] All apocalypses in some way reflect a crisis situation and seek to assure those alienated from the power structures and suffering for their religious beliefs that salvation is theirs.[26]

In his study of the sociopolitical conditions of first-century Palestine, **Richard Horsley** takes issue with this view of apocalyptic, and with the negative presuppositions with which many scholars approach it. Rather than being sects bent on overthrowing the dominant society, they were people who saw themselves as righteous believers and upholders of biblical traditions. *Anomie* has been used as a description of the conditions engendering apocalyptic movement; Horsley insists that chaos is not the problem, but too much rule, in this case, rule of an alien and oppressive sort. Apocalypticism is not a retreat or alienation from history, and its adherents view the situation as having historical significance of the highest order.[27]

In the context of Israel, the role of apocalyptic was first of all remembering the blessings of God and his previous redemptive acts in the face of oppression and injustice; creative envisioning of a just world free from oppression; and "critical demystifying of the pretensions and practices of the established order." The apocalyptic imagination, then, strengthened and encouraged people to endure and acted as an impetus to resistance and revolt.[28]

It is questionable whether apocalyptic is a retreat from history or human involvement. Rather, it is an alternate reading of history and a call for involvement, and presupposes a worldview very different from our own.

Christopher Rowland's approach to apocalyptic differs somewhat in its emphasis. For Rowland, the revelation of divine secrets is the essential element of apocalyptic. His approach has the advantage of taking the religious and spiritual experience of the apocalypticists seriously. Apocalyptic is revelatory, illuminating the recipient with an unveiled glimpse of reality.

Apocalyptic is an answer to the desperate entreaty of Isaiah 64, in which God is asked to come down and solve for us the many riddles of life in this world. The seer is able to mediate God's secrets concerning the world and human destiny, and since they are definitive and incontrovertible answers, human questioning is futile. In possession of these divine secrets and an understanding of the nature of reality, people can organize their lives accordingly.[29]

The essential element of apocalyptic is the revelation of divine mysteries and heavenly truth. Eschatological elements are often found in apocalyptic, but their presence is not necessary because eschatology is not definitive. The use of the term *apocalyptic* as a synonym of eschatology must be avoided, as this can obscure the revelatory nature of this genre, especially with regard to matters other than eschatology.[30]

It is certainly true that *apocalyptic* must not be used as a synonym for *eschatology;* however, it must also be recognized that *apocalyptic* was not just about any heavenly mystery but about God's plan for humanity, his justice, vindication of the just, and punishment of the wicked.[31]

Philip Vielhauer's apocalyptic consists of a general mindset that includes the following: (1) the two-ages dualism that is temporal rather than absolute or metaphysical; (2) pessimism and otherworldly hope; (3) universalism and individualism, in that apocalyptic operates on a cosmic scale. In the events of the resurrection, world judgment, and world dissolution, the individual no longer is identified with a collective such as race or ethnic group; and (4) determinism and imminent expectation of the kingdom of God, which involves the periodization of history and calculations concerning its end. Vielhauer's definition is not precise enough for evaluating specific works or passages.[32]

All of these studies offered helpful and illuminating insights, and the direction of research moved toward greater precision and rigor. No single one of them, however, was sufficient. There was a need for a paradigm that would incorporate the fruits of past research and yet meet the needs of future studies. The Society of Biblical Literature Genres Project published its results in 1979 in volume 14 of *Semeia.* In the SBL study, all of the texts classified as apocalypses from the time period 250 B.C.E. to 250 C.E. were analyzed, resulting in a master paradigm composed of two sections dealing with the framework of the revelation and its content, which in turn is divided into the manner of the revelation's conveyance and the concluding elements.

In this study, **John J. Collins** describes two broad types of apocalypses, historical and heavenly ascents. Daniel characterizes the first type, Enoch the second. The content includes both historical and eschatological events on a temporal axis and otherworldly beings and places on a spatial one. Each of the two types was divided into three subtypes based on their eschatology, which Collins in a later study deemed of lesser importance for the study of the genre. Collins defines the genre as follows:

> "Apocalypse" is a genre of revelatory literature with a narrative framework, in which a revelation is mediated by an otherworldly being to a human recipient, disclosing a transcendent reality which is both temporal, insofar as it envisages eschatological salvation, and spatial, insofar as it involves another, supernatural world.[33]

The 1979 definition was criticized as being ahistorical and lacking a description of function. He accepted a refinement of the definition from **Adela Yarbro Collins** in a 1986 Semeia study, so that it now reads:

> "Apocalypse" is a genre of revelatory literature with a narrative framework, in which a revelation is mediated by an otherworldly being to a human recipient, disclosing a transcendent reality which is both temporal, insofar as it envisages eschatological salvation, and spatial, insofar as it involves another, supernatural world; such a work *is intended to interpret present, earthly circumstances in light of the supernatural world and of the future, and to influence both the understanding and the behavior of the audience by means of divine authority.*[34] (Italics mine)

One can then distinguish between true apocalyptic material and oracles, dreams, and visions that lack these characteristics. According to Collins, this definition applies to various sections of 1 Enoch, Daniel, 4 Ezra, 2 Baruch, Apocalypse of Abraham, 3 Baruch, 2 Enoch, Testament of Levi 2—5, the fragmentary

Apocalypse of Zephaniah 1, and with some qualification to Jubilees and the Testament of Abraham. It also applies to a fairly wide body of Christian and Gnostic literature and to some Persian and Greco-Roman material.[35]

There have been a number of challenges in recent years to the prevailing interpretive model. Some have questioned whether apocalyptic can even be defined. One of the areas of contention is the relationship of apocalyptic genre and eschatology, and whether eschatology is constitutive of apocalyptic. Would it be possible to have an apocalypse without the presence of eschatology? Secondly, the whole notion of apocalyptic being resistance literature written and read by persecuted and marginalized groups has been questioned (see discussion of the Book of Revelation).[36]

In his 1996 work, **D. S. Sim** indicates that he would prefer a clear distinction between the apocalyptic genre, and apocalyptic eschatology and apocalypticism. He takes issue with Collins by denying that there is necessarily a relationship between apocalyptic eschatology and the apocalyptic genre. He points out that several apocalypses, such as 2 Enoch and 3 Baruch, do not contain much eschatological material at all, focusing instead on the heavenly world, cosmology, and astronomy. Sim even contemplates a new name for apocalyptic eschatology.[37]

In his study of 1 Enoch, **G. W. E. Nickelsburg** outlines the apocalyptic worldview, which exhibits a dualism between the divine beings and humans, the vertical and horizontal planes, as well as the present age and the new age. Human beings live at the intersection of all of these dualisms, and revelation, which is the essential element of apocalyptic, offers a vision that helps people to understand and bridge the dualisms inherent in reality and their experience.[38]

Martha Himmelfarb studies revelation, rapture, and transformation of the apocalyptic seers and concludes that these visions, especially those involving angels, is an attempt to overcome the perceived distance between God and humans and, rather than pessimism, it reflects a hopeful or optimistic note.[39]

Collins points out that although apocalypses contain and reveal many things, such as wisdom instructions, halachic rulings, and cosmological data, they are always subordinate to the relationship between the supernatural world and the eschatological expectation. He insists on retaining *apocalypse* as a broad term that is inclusive enough to embrace different subgroups.[40]

Apocalyptic Symbolism

M. Eugene Boring clarifies the nature of symbolism and language in a very helpful fashion, and in general, his distinctions are shared by most scholars. Boring makes a distinction between the two types of language, propositional and pictorial. The first, propositional, is logical, diachronic in that everything is laid out in a logical, chronological progression, and objectifying in nature. This type of language contrasts myth with truth. Symbols are only seen as steno-symbols; that is, a one-to-one correspondence with an object, person, or event.

Pictorial language, on the other hand, communicates meaning, rather than scientific knowledge. A fine example of this is the symbolism used in the creation accounts in Genesis 1—3. Pictorial language is nonobjectifying and does not teach doctrine. It points beyond, to ultimate reality, and the reader/hearer is invited to participation rather than mere observance.

The symbols used in Revelation are of the second type and are tensive and polyvalent. They are not steno-symbols, code, or allegory, and are not meant to conceal anything. In fact, just the opposite is true: they communicate that which cannot be expressed in any other way. Being tensive means that they evoke a plurality of meanings; no one interpretation is exhaustive. Pictorial language is not informational or logical. Its synchronic nature means that symbols that would clash logically are allowed to exist simultaneously. Finally, rather than being contrasted with truth, myth is its vehicle.[41] The real problem is when a book like Revelation is analyzed according to the norms of propositional language. In a sense, the text is asked to do that for which it was never intended, and to deliver information which it cannot bear. The real power of the symbols lies in their tensive and non-logical nature.

Conclusion

Knowing the genre of a particular book, chapter, or passage is the key for discerning the intended message. We do not turn to poetry or mythology for scientific information or vice versa (although each contains elements of the other!). A correct apocalyptic interpretation of critical passages of the New Testament can influence the interpretation and development of doctrine, Christology, ecclesiology, and ethics.

Caution must be taken not to present a caricature of apocalyptic, detaching it almost completely from history, time, and earthly categories. Although some of these elements are indeed present in varying degrees, the contrast between prophecy and apocalyptic is not stark and absolute. In apocalyptic, history is still the playing field for the divine/human drama that is unfolding, but the decisive moves will definitely be from above. Although the call of apocalyptic was to the individual, it was understood in both Jewish and Christian apocalyptic that one's membership in the assembly of Israel was crucial, thereby creating a tension between communal and individual salvation, rather than opposition.

The modified SBL paradigm is the standard model with which to analyze apocalyptic texts. Keeping in mind Hanson's caution that such models are merely a useful heuristic device, we can avoid being overly rigid or devoting too much time to endless refinements of the definition or even new models. Most of the descriptions of apocalyptic characteristics are correct, but relying on a broader, more generic definition leaves room for variations within the genre. It is safe to say that some of the more salient characteristics include a sharp contrast between two ages, an expectation of imminent and dramatic decisive events, often in the form of cosmic upheaval and/or reversal in the social order, and vindication of the just. Its purpose is to give hope and encouragement to those who are suffering persecution or oppression, but it also serves to enlist people for God's cause, for the demand to orient one's life toward God is immediate and uncompromising.

2
Jesus and the End of the Ages

Truly, I tell you, there are some standing here who will not taste death before they see the Son of Man coming in his kingdom. (Matt 16:28)

These and similar passages have long been a source of theological difficulty. If Jesus did utter these words, why have they not come to pass? In fact, it appears that they cannot—that generation has long ago tasted death. In the "little apocalypse" in Mark 13:5–37 (=Matt 24:4–36; Luke 21:8–36) Jesus prophesies the destruction of the Temple and Jerusalem. Most scholars look upon these predictions as after-the-fact *(ex eventu)* prophecies and doubt that they derive from the historical Jesus, at least in their present form. Do the apocalyptic statements and pronouncements in the New Testament reflect the beliefs and teachings of the historical Jesus, or are they the product of the early church? This is one of the most vexing and contentious questions in New Testament and historical Jesus research. This question is more than just a curiosity, for it impacts theology, Christology, and ethics. Was Jesus a teacher of wisdom sayings or an apocalyptic prophet?

The Q Source—Witness to a Different Jesus?

Central to all New Testament research is the source schol-ars call "Q," which stands for the German word *Quelle* or source. It is the symbol scholars since the nineteenth century have used to describe common material found in Matthew and Luke, but not in Mark. Most assume that this was a document source that is no longer extant—no one has ever seen Q. **John Kloppenborg** and other researchers believe that they can dis-sect the Q source into different layers and show its development over time. Q itself is a composite document and a deliberate lit-erary creation. There has also been an increasing tendency to refer to it not merely as a document or source, but as a Gospel in its own right, perhaps representing a layer of tradition more primitive than the canonical Gospels.[1] This is an important point, because the reconstructed Q lacks a passion narrative or resurrection accounts, so there are some who theorize that these elements of our tradition might not have played a prominent role in some early Christian communities, and this has profound implications for Christian theology.[2]

Although the existence of Q enjoys the support of a schol-arly consensus, it is not by any means unanimous, for there are those who suggest other means to explain the parallel passages in Matthew and Luke.[3]

A debated point is whether the earliest layers of Q contain apocalyptic material, and reconstructions of the historical Jesus often draw on Q research to bolster a nonapocalyptic Jesus. In fact, Kloppenborg does not deny that the earliest layers contain apocalyptic material. He states that many key elements of apoca-lyptic are either absent or attenuated. He suggests that the com-munity that generated Q used apocalyptic language to solidify communal boundaries and destabilize perceptions of the world in order to prepare people for the teachings of Jesus.

The Son of Man

The term "Son of Man" is associated with the apocalyptic passages in the Synoptic Gospels. The question of their meaning and authenticity is important for the reconstruction of the historical Jesus. In the NT Synoptic Gospels, there are seventy-four instances of the phrase "Son of Man," forming thirty-seven distinct sayings, with one occurrence in the Gospel of Thomas.[4] The Q source contains Son of Man sayings at all levels of its composition, and sayings or allusions are also present in Mark, John, and the Book of Revelation.[5] There are places in the Synoptic Gospels where the term in used in a generic, nonapocalyptic sense, as in Matthew 8:20/Luke 9:58, where Jesus states that "foxes have holes and birds of the air have nests, but the son of man has nowhere to lay his head." In other places, however, it is used in a distinctly apocalyptic sense denoting drastic change and cosmic upheaval, as in Mark 13:24–26: "…they will see 'the Son of Man coming in clouds' with great power and glory."[6]

Adela Yarbro Collins believes that it is likely that Jesus spoke of the heavenly Son of Man and associated his teachings and mission with the one thought to be a heavenly being or angel, although he did not associate himself with that being. He used the definite form (the Son of Man) as a way of alluding to the Daniel text, which was already known to his audience. After his death, his followers, believing him to be in an exalted state, associated him with that heavenly being. Collins disagrees with the conclusions of many scholars that the Son of Man was not a Jewish title and that there was no widespread expectation of the coming of a celestial being of that title. She points to use of the image and title in the Similitudes of Enoch (1 Enoch 37—71), and the fact that it would have been more likely for the followers of Jesus to have identified him with this figure if Jesus had already made some sort of association.[7]

John J. Collins, on the other hand, sees no reason why Jesus could not have applied at least the term to himself, as the text from

Daniel was widely known and was drawn upon for similar apocalyptic scenarios in the Similitudes of Enoch and 4 Ezra.[8]

An Apocalyptic Jesus—A Jewish Jesus

E. P. Sanders is probably best known for his epochal work, *Paul and Palestinian Judaism,* which was instrumental in overturning many of the prejudices and caricatures of Judaism. His analysis of the Gospels in *Jesus and Judaism* places Jesus within Judaism and adhering to its "covenantal nomism," and he firmly rejects any interpretation that attempts to contrast Jesus with Judaism or portray him as its antithesis.[9] His thesis is that "Jesus is to be positively connected with the hope for Jewish restoration," and he sees "Jewish eschatology" and "restoration of Israel" as virtually synonymous,[10] considering the combination of restoration and reversal peculiar to Palestinian Jewish apocalypses.[11] The restoration was to be a new order created by God and would include the reconstitution of the twelve tribes, a new temple, the inclusion of the Gentiles, sinners, and social outcasts.[12] This restoration eschatology is the connecting link between the intentions of Jesus, his death, and the rise of the movement named after him. The disciples continued to expect the occurrence of this restoration.[13]

This view is reflected in what he holds to be the indisputable facts: Jesus was baptized by John, he thought of the inner circle of his followers in terms of the "Twelve," and he took action against the Temple that predicted (or threatened) its destruction. The Temple and twelve are national symbols, which indicate clearly that he expected the restoration of Israel.[14]

Sanders focuses his study on the Temple incident, which he deems historical at least in essence, and the event that contributed to the death of Jesus. In Christian tradition, this has been called the "cleansing" of the Temple, and he illustrates why that is not the case. The sacrifices were ordained by God, and the buying and selling of the sacrificial animals a necessary corollary. This was the purpose of the Temple, and there is no evidence that Jesus sought to abolish its sacrificial activities. Many groups, such as the Essenes, railed against the corruption of the priests, but the NT passages contain no such criticisms. If Jesus predicted or threatened the destruction of the Temple and its rebuilding after three days, and Sanders believes that in some form this is likely, then it would have been the prediction of the imminent arrival of the judgment and the new age.[15]

The strength of Sanders' analysis lies in the fact that it places Jesus squarely within the Jewish milieu of the first century as a participant, rather than using the "Jewish background" as a foil for Jesus to criticize or overturn. His Jesus makes sense in a Jewish context, although many will disagree with his view of the person and mission of Jesus.

Paula Fredriksen insists that Jesus has to be intelligible to his first-century audience.[16] She agrees with most of the points made by Sanders with the exception of one important one: She denies the historicity of the Temple incident. Since the Gospel of John places this event at the beginning of Jesus' ministry and Paul is completely silent about it, she concludes that if it occurred at all, it was a free-floating tradition without context and was not the cause of his arrest.[17]

She touches on a number of facts: The movement settled in Jerusalem instead of Galilee despite the fact that Jesus was preaching peasant equality. Gentiles did not play a prominent role during the ministry of Jesus, but they were included in the movement after his death. Paul and Mark both proclaim that the Kingdom of God is coming. Paul is still confident despite the delay—note Romans 13:11 where he says that it is even closer than when we first believed. Even twenty years later, Mark is repeating something already seen not to be true. It would be unlikely that they would invent an embarrassing tradition. He had an inner core of followers called the Twelve, who continued to spread the Gospel throughout the Diaspora after his death. All of these facts, she states, can be explained by Jewish apocalyptic expectation.[18]

Further evidence of the apocalyptic nature of the proclamation of Jesus abounds. For instance, the prohibition of divorce in Matthew 19:10–12 ends with the statement that some make themselves eunuchs for the sake of the Kingdom of God. Paul's command in 1 Corinthians 7 for married and single people to remain as they are because the time is short and the world is passing away is clearly framed in apocalyptic terms. The Eucharist itself is evidence of the Kingdom, and Jesus speaks of the Kingdom in connection with it in Mark 14:22–25, as does Paul in 1 Corinthians 11.[19]

If the temple incident was not the cause of his death, what was? Jesus had preached the coming of the apocalyptic Kingdom of God to crowds already steeped in first-century apocalyptic and messianic expectations. The ethic preached in the Sermon on the Mount, especially nonresistance to evil, further illustrate this point. He probably proclaimed that the Kingdom was at hand while in Jerusalem, and the hysterical crowds began to proclaim him Messiah. Pilate—possibly at the prompting of the priests—killed him because of the threat of the crowds and fear of further unrest. His resurrection was seen as an apocalyptic event, for resurrection was a redemptive act expected at the End of Days. This explains why his disciples continued to operate from an apocalyptic model.[20]

Although her book is helpful in many ways, Fredriksen's argument concerning the Temple incident is unconvincing. She focuses on the immense size of the Temple and how unnoticeable and insignificant an incident such as the one described in the Gospels would have been. The symbolic action would have been incompressible to anyone outside Jesus' immediate group. Therefore, the priests had no reason to feel threatened, for the Temple was not in any danger. This, however, is a rationalization two thousand years after the event. Jerusalem was and still is a volatile flashpoint, and in such a religiously supercharged atmosphere as Jerusalem at Passover time, seemingly insignificant actions can have explosive and catastrophic results.

N. T. Wright confronts what he feels is the chief problem with many past works on the eschatological Jesus: An eschatological Jesus confined to his own time is not relevant to ours. For Wright, much of the problem lies with definition. When we ask the question, "Did Jesus expect the end of the world?" do we mean the time-space continuum? He holds that not only is it unnecessary to interpret apocalyptic language in this fashion, it is necessary as historians that we not do so. Apocalyptic language is an "elaborate metaphor-system for investing historical events with theological significance."[21]

Eschatology, according to Wright, is the climax of Israel's history, and the significance of the events soon to occur can only be adequately expressed in "end of the world" language. It is important to emphasize that these events are to take place within spatial and chronological history.[22]

The action of Jesus in the Temple, then, is a symbolic act signifying its destruction. Its subsequent destruction, along with the resurrection of Jesus, were both seen as vindications of his claims and actions. In the background of this event is the Maccabean revolt and Daniel 7 and 9, especially the abomination of desolation. There is a call to repentance as Jesus the Messiah predicts the destruction of the Temple and city in Mark 13. Apocalyptic language is the appropriate mode of expression for such events.[23]

In a volume of collected essays criticizing Jesus and the victory of God, **Dale Allison** parts company with Wright on the matter of the nature of apocalyptic language. Wright denies that the end of the time-space universe was intended by apocalyptic language. Allison demonstrates through examples from the ancient literature of the Jews that they indeed believed that these writings referred to events in the physical and historical plane, although such works could at the same time be symbolic. There is no reason to read modern views back into the texts, and he suspects that Wright has sidestepped the theological difficulties created by an apocalyptic Jesus by utilizing a nonliteral interpretation of the texts.[24]

A Nonapocalyptic Jesus

In a 1986 essay, **Marcus Borg** discussed some of the elements of NT research that were undermining the old consensus of an eschatological Jesus.[25] This had been the bedrock of NT research since Schweitzer, with Bultmann, Bornkamm, and many others basing their works on that assumption. Newer research had brought the authenticity of the "Coming Son of Man" sayings into serious doubt. Additionally, there is increasing agreement that the "Son of Man" was not a first-century Jewish designation for a supernatural or end-of-the-world figure. Finally, **Geza Vermes** argues that "Son of Man" in Aramaic had no pre-Christian titular usage and was a common idiom and would not have had any particular significance for listeners.[26] Vermes leads those who believe that the NT Son of Man sayings that derive from the historical Jesus were instances of Jesus using a circumlocution for the sake of modesty.[27]

Without Son of Man sayings, Borg holds, there is no reason to associate Kingdom of God with the end of the world, and imagery to that effect is present only in the Son of Man sayings. The inference is drawn from the event of the resurrection and in connection with expectation of the return of Jesus.[28]

Borg clarified some of his positions in a later essay. First of all, he believes that Jesus certainly had held and expressed on occasion some eschatological beliefs. He merely denies that imminent eschatology should be the interpretive context for reading the Jesus tradition.[29] Jesus was also concerned about the future, and threatened the Temple in the manner of the OT prophets. He envisioned an alternative social entity for Israel's future. There was also a strong sense of urgency in the Jesus tradition. Finally, the apocalyptic understanding of the Jesus tradition was generated through the Easter experience, with an intensification of eschatological expectation around the year 70 C.E., the time of the revolt and the destruction of the temple.[30]

John Dominic Crossan's *The Historical Jesus: The Life of a Mediterranean Jewish Peasant* has been extremely influential not only for historical Jesus studies, but for the whole issue of the nature and origin of apocalyptic in the New Testament.

Crossan applies cross-cultural and cross-temporal anthropology as well as Hellenistic or Greco-Roman history to his method. Additionally, he is willing to include many sources outside the canonical scriptures; indeed, they are at least for the purpose of study placed on an equal footing. He makes a careful catalogue of sources and sorts them according to temporal stratification into four broad categories. The four categories are: 30–60 C.E.; 60–80 C.E.; 80–120 C.E.; and 120–150 C.E.[31] This is the point where his methodology is most vulnerable to criticism, for many of the extracanonical sources cannot be dated with any degree of surety, and there is a broad spectrum of scholarly opinion. In addition to the genuine Pauline letters, the first stratum, 30–60 C.E., contains the Gospel of Thomas, the Gospel of the Hebrews, several papyri, and the Q source. These latter sources are crucial for Crossan's reconstruction, and moving them just a few years later on the spectrum would alter some results. Crossan has been criticized with basing too much of his reconstruction on assumptions and speculations regarding dating, purpose, and provenance.[32]

Crossan agrees with Borg's definition of *eschatological* in that it includes "as an indispensable element the notion that the world itself will come to an end, including the traditional expectation of last judgment, resurrection, and dawn of the new age." He goes on to say that "the eschatological Jesus is one who thought this was imminent. Thus, with the term 'eschatological,' I do not mean 'end' in more metaphorical senses, either in the sense of a dramatic change in Israel's history, or in the sense of a radical change in the individual's sensitivity which one might describe by speaking of the (old) world coming to an end for that individual." He differs, however, in his insistence that this describes the apocalyptic Jesus and that eschatology is a "wider and generic term for world-negation extending from apocalyptic eschatology...through mystical or utopian modes, and on to ascetical, libertarian, or anarchistic possibilities. In other words, all apocalyptic is eschatological, but not all eschatology is apocalyptic."[33] This distinction is important, because although Crossan will deny that Jesus is apocalyptic in his preaching and message, he will affirm that Jesus is eschatological, which he defines as world-negation. This would be a "radical criticism of culture and civilization and thus a fundamental rejection of this world's values and expectations."[34] This term would describe all those who turn away from the world out of grief, pain, anger, or despair and imagine a better or perfect world that puts the present one to shame. This world-negation can be expressed in mystical, utopian, ascetic, libertarian, or anarchistic eschatologies.

One of the key arguments used by those who hold that Jesus was an apocalyptic prophet is his link with John the Baptist. Jesus was baptized by John the Baptist and was probably his disciple. John the Baptist was an apocalyptic prophet; therefore Jesus was almost certainly one himself. Crossan attempts to demolish that argument with a detailed analysis of three groups of texts: Gospel of Thomas 78 and Q in Matthew 11:7b–9/Luke 7:24b–26; Gospel of Thomas 46 and Q in Matthew 11:11/Luke 7:28; Mark 2:18–20 and Q in Matthew 11:18–19/Luke 7:33–34. He concludes that there Jesus is distancing himself from the apocalyptic and ascetical ministry of John.[35]

It appears that Jesus frequently foretold the coming of the Son of Man, which is certainly an apocalyptic entity. He acknowledges that when Jesus uses the term in the Gospels, it appears to be a title describing a transcendental agent of divine judgment. The question Crossan then asks is whether this derives from the historical Jesus, or is it a later addition? After an analysis of the Son of Man texts, Crossan concludes that Jesus never used the term in any titular sense. He states that "in the entire Son of Man tradition there is only a single instance where two independent sources have the expression in more than a single version." In those places where the term is found "it is one but not the other version, and it always looks as if it is coming in later rather than having been there from the start."[36]

Crossan believes that "Son of Man" as the title of an apocalyptic judge did not arise from the historical Jesus or even all elements of the early Christian community. He points out that the apocalyptic portions of Paul, the Didache, and the Gospel of Thomas all contain allusions to Daniel 7:13, but do not mention the Son of Man. He explains its early genesis in the Christian tradition as the result of texts in which Jesus uses the phrase in its generic sense, that is, either referring to humankind or to himself, which in turn made the transition from Jesus as an apocalyptic judge to Jesus as the Son of Man, both stemming from Daniel 7:13.[37] His final conclusion is that John the Baptist was an apocalyptic prophet who prepared his followers for the imminent arrival of God, but Jesus, who initially accepted this vision, changed his views after the execution of John and in his own preaching, made a clear contrast between John's vision and his own. He never spoke of himself as the apocalyptic Son of Man.[38]

Crossan concludes that Jesus was a peasant Jewish Cynic, a sort of itinerant counter-cultural teacher of wisdom. He lived close to the Greco-Roman city of Sepphoris and possibly had access to Cynicism. His work was centered on the farms and villages of Lower Galilee, and his program consisted of free healing and common eating, a "religious and economic egalitarianism that negated alike and at once the hierarchical and patronal normalcies of Jewish religion and Roman power."[39]

Jesus the Apocalyptic Prophet

Bart Ehrman's book defends at least the essence of Schweitzer's position that Jesus was an apocalyptic prophet. Ruling out extrabiblical sources and noncanonical Gospels, and viewing Q with caution, he concludes that the canonical Gospels provide us with the best historically reliable information.[40]

What does Jesus mean in his historical context? In review-
ing the political and social situation of first-century C.E. Palestine,
he notes reality was defined by the political and economic domination of Rome. Various sects and parties in Palestine dealt with
that reality in diverse ways; one response shared by many of these
groups was apocalypticism.[41]

Following the rules he laid down for reconstruction, he
notes that Q, Mark, and the portions particular to Matthew and
Luke all portray Jesus as apocalyptic in his words and actions.
These are the earliest layers of tradition. The Gospel of John and
the Gospel of Thomas do not portray him in a similar fashion. The
later a document, the more the apocalypticism of Jesus is attenuated. An apocalyptic prophet as a model for Jesus meets all the
criteria for authenticity: multiple independent attestation, as
above; dissimilarity, as some of the ways he talked about the end
did not coincide with later belief (e.g., Mark 8:38 and Matt 25);
and contextual credibility, in a first-century apocalyptic milieu.[42]

The link between Jesus and John the Baptist is clear indica-
tion of the nature of Jesus' preaching. At the beginning of his ministry, Jesus was baptized by John the Baptist, who was clearly an
apocalyptic prophet and whose message was the approach of
destruction, judgment, and the coming of the Kingdom. The communities after the death of Jesus were apocalyptic in belief, as in 1
Thessalonians and 1 Corinthians. Ehrman concludes that Jesus
himself was the link between these two poles and was a Jewish
apocalypticist.[43]

But the teachings of Jesus themselves also attest to his apocalyptic message. The Kingdom of God enjoys a central role in his
proclamation, and this signals the approaching judgment of the
Gentiles and the destruction of the world order (cf. Mark 8:38;
13:24–27; Luke 17:24–30/Matt 24:27, 37–39). The coming of the
Son of Man, the reversal of the social order, the requirement to
become like children to enter the Kingdom, and the approaching
destruction are all indicators of apocalyptic intent. The radical
nature of the discipleship expected of his followers was similar to

that proclaimed in the Beatitudes. The command to leave all, to hate one's family and parents, to give everything away and share one's property, are all in preparation for the Kingdom. Absolute commitment is required, and people began implementing now in small ways (note the parables of the mustard seed, etc.) what will be fully manifested later. Even his association with the socially marginalized, such as women, the physically imperfect, and sinners were signs of the coming reversal of the social order and the arrival of God's Kingdom. Jesus probably did prophesy the destruction of the Temple, as had many of the prophets.[44]

Dale Allison takes a firm stance against Crossan's claim that many so-called apocalyptic elements in the Gospels are not authentic. He especially zeros in on Crossan's use of Q for much of his reconstruction. He points out that the reconstruction of Q's history is hypothetical, and even if the earlier layer of Q is non-apocalyptic, it does not follow that it is more authentic.[45]

Allison notes a number of apocalyptic elements and symbols in the Gospels. The restoration of Israel figures very strongly in the tradition, with Luke 22:28–30 referring to judging the tribes of Israel and Luke 13:28–29 stating that many will come from the east and the west, which probably envisions the ingathering of Israel. Eschatological tribulation is present in much of the preaching of Jesus. The symbol of fire is used in Luke 12:39–50 and 51–53. The harvest, threshing, and winnowing, as in Luke 3:17; Mark 4:2–9, 26–29; and Luke 10:12, all have parallels in 4 Ezra 4:30, 39; Revelation 14:14–16; and 2 Baruch 70:2. Luke 10:21,23 and Mark 4:11 refer to secrets hidden and revealed only to the simple or elect. Both Jeremiah 31:34 and Habakkuk 2:14 claim that in the end, there will be an outpouring of the knowledge of God. The revelation of divine secrets is also referred to as an eschatological event in the Dead Sea Scrolls, as in 1QpHab11:1. Finally, the prohibition of divorce and the amplification of the Law of Moses both reflect an end-time ethical urgency and a time when the end will match the beginning, that is, a recapitulation.[46]

Much has been made of contradictions in the Gospels between statements that imply that the end is in the future and those that speak of the end or Kingdom as having arrived. Additionally, despite the stringent demands of the apocalyptic passages, there appears to be an assumption that life will continue. Allison observes that eschatological thinking is by nature nonrational and that tensions and contradictions are inherent. He cites numerous examples from the Book of Jubilees, Paul, Daniel, and 1 Enoch to illustrate that apocalyptic prophets could speak of the end as having arrived and yet be far off, and continue to make provisions for the future. Jesus perhaps thought of himself as being in the middle of the unfolding of the eschatological scenario, and for this Allison coins the term "inaugurated eschatology."[47]

His principal reasons for viewing Jesus as an apocalyptic prophet are manifold. Jesus lived in an apocalyptic milieu, and both the Old Testament and the extrabiblical Jewish works of the time were laden with apocalyptic eschatology and symbolism. It was part of the expectation of the imminent redemption of Israel. Apocalyptic views were held by most early Christians, as is apparent in the Acts of the Apostles, 1 and 2 Thessalonians, 1 and 2 Corinthians, and so on. It would seem to follow that these communities based their eschatological expectations on the teachings of Jesus, and Allison disagrees with Crossan for setting Jesus and John the Baptist against each other. The Synoptics, as in Mark 9:1 and 13:30, regard the Kingdom of God as near, and tell believers to look for the return of the Lord or Son of Man. In ancient Jewish literature, the Kingdom of God is associated with both imminence and eschatology, as is apparent in the statements of Jesus about the Kingdom of God in Mark 10:23; 14:25; Luke 13:29 (Q); 11:2 (Q). There was a common Jewish conviction about the latter days that God would finally defeat Satan and the forces of evil (cf. Jub 2:29; 1 En 10:4–6; 54:4–6). Despite its moral focus, the Jesus tradition does not give guidance for changing political or social realities, or offer human solutions to concrete problems. It looks forward to God to set things right. Finally, the death and resurrection of Jesus is connected with eschatological texts, such as Zechariah and Amos, as in Matthew 27:51–53. When Jesus was alive, Luke 19:11 tells us that the disciples supposed that the Kingdom of God was to appear immediately. When he was killed and then seen alive again, their expectations and their experiences matched.

Taking issue with Crossan and others and their assertion that Jesus was certainly no ascetic, Allison builds a detailed and sustained argument showing that he did practice and preach asceticism and that this is closely linked with his apocalyptic eschatology. Sexual continence, renunciation of families and businesses, self-denial were all elements common to eschatological movements of the time, such as that of the Essenes, as well as millenarian movements throughout history. Jesus tells some of his followers to give up their property and money, to embark on missionary journeys without essentials, and to not even look upon a woman with lustful intent. These directives should be understood as eschatological preparation. The stringent demands made by Jesus in the Synoptic Gospels should not surprise us, nor should we look for evidence of contempt for the world or foreign influences.[48]

Asceticism and renunciation, then, are part and parcel of eschatological expectation. Both the Gospels and Paul enjoin sexual continence in preparation for the age to come. In 1 Corinthians 11, the Eucharist itself is viewed as an eschatological sign, and the dim view of marriage in 1 Corinthians 7 can only be understood in an apocalyptic context: The end is too close to worry about the distraction of marriage.[49] The asceticism of Jesus should not be viewed as a form of dualism or Stoicism, but as dedication to an eschatological mission, distance from the present world order, rhetorical persuasion, and a sign of approaching judgment.[50]

Conclusion

Where do these many works of research leave us? Although it is true that we cannot simply take the Gospels at face value and that they contain theological embellishments and retrojection of post-70 events into the account of the life of Jesus, the bulk of evidence indicates that Jesus shared the apocalyptic worldview of many of his contemporaries. The letters of Paul (see chapter 3) were written nearly a generation before the Gospels and only twenty years after the death of Jesus, and they clearly express an apocalyptic expectation. When the Gospels were written, the events predicted in the apocalyptic portions, with the exception of the destruction of the Temple, had still not taken place. It would have been in the theological interests of the early church to downplay or even eliminate apocalyptic statements. Only in the Gospels of Luke and John do we see attenuation, but not elimination, of apocalyptic predictions. This suggests that they at least have their roots in the teachings of the historical Jesus and were modified in the various Gospels to reflect the theological concerns of the evangelists and the delay of the parousia.

3
Paul's "Apocalyptic Gospel"

Paul's letters have always been challenging and even frustrating to exegetes and biblical theologians. Many passages seem contradictory; Paul can often be quoted against Paul. One can see this especially when his statements in Galatians and Romans concerning the status of Israel and the Law are compared. His writings seem to defy systemization, and our post-Enlightenment mania for consistency and order in matters intellectual is often thwarted by the man from Tarsus. Since the Reformation, Protestant scholars have held justification by faith to be the abiding core of Paul's theology, while Catholics have concentrated on unity of faith and doctrine, but recent Pauline studies have raised many questions.

Apocalyptic eschatology and symbols are found in the Pauline letters in several places. Two very clear examples are 1 Thessalonians 4:5–12 and 2 Thessalonians 2:1–12 (although many scholars believe 2 Thess to be written by someone other than Paul). Both letters in the Corinthian correspondence contain apocalyptic elements: 1 Corinthians 4:1; 2:6–8; 7:29–31; 15:20–28, 51–52; 2 Corinthians 12:1–12. In the Letter to the Romans, 13:11–14 is clearly an apocalyptic exhortation. There is some disagreement, however, as to the extent that apocalyptic theology and outlook affects Paul's entire theology. Some would still prefer to say that Paul uses apocalyptic language at times, but is not apocalyptic in his worldview.

Schweitzer Revisited

Albert Schweitzer once again is the point of departure. In Paul's theology and eschatology, he does not simply look to a future redemption, but believes that through a mystical "being-in-Christ" one can experience the future as it is realized in the present. The natural world of the previous age and the transcendental new age intermingle in the present. This is in many respects a consequence of his eschatology, which Schweitzer portrays as deviating sharply from that of Jesus. Jesus, according to Schweitzer, lives entirely from the Son-of-Man eschatology of the Book of Daniel and Enoch.[1]

Schweitzer believes that Paul accepted the eschatological views of Baruch and Ezra in which he was trained. This is reflected in 1 Corinthians 15, where he states that the last enemy, death, will only be destroyed at the end of the Messianic Kingdom. Following the reasoning of Baruch and Ezra, the elect enjoy both the temporary messianic blessedness and the eternal one, which begins after the end of the Messianic Kingdom. Those who were unfortunate enough to die before the time of the Messiah can only attain the eternal blessedness and must remain dead during the Messianic Kingdom. But in classical eschatology, the Messiah was assumed to have come before the arrival of the Kingdom. In 1 Thessalonians 4:13–18, he must deal with the problem of believers who die before the parousia. This forces Paul to modify his eschatology, and these changes are somewhat contradictory and lie somewhere in between the eschatology of the scribes and that of Jesus. He claims that those who are the elect already enjoy the resurrection mode of existence through the agency of the spirit. The elect of the final generation, even those who have already died, will be able to participate in the Kingdom by means of the resurrection.[2] This occurs, claims Schweitzer, through two resurrections. In the first, dead believers in Christ are raised in order to enjoy the benefits of the Messianic Kingdom; the second resurrection, all human beings who have ever lived are raised for the final divine judgment and the apportioning of eternal life or punishment.[3] This doctrine of a double resurrection was an innovation, since all previous eschatology spoke of only one. He reached this conclusion not from the teachings of Jesus, but from the fact of his death and resurrection.

The unforeseen event that caused so much rethinking of the traditional eschatology was the appearance of the Messiah before the Messianic Age and his death and resurrection. But the resurrection of Jesus had released supernatural powers into the world that were already at work. The natural and the supernatural, then, are intermingled during the interval between the resurrection and return of Jesus, and those who live "in Christ" and who enjoy the fruits of the spirit are acutely aware of that.

> While other believers held that the finger of the world-clock was touching on the beginning of the coming hour and were waiting for the stroke that would announce this, Paul told them that it had already passed beyond the point, and that they had failed to hear the striking of the hour, which in fact struck at the Resurrection of Jesus.[4]

Schweitzer admires Paul as a thinker and indeed looks upon him as the father of innovative Christian thought. He frees the belief in Jesus as the coming Messiah from its temporal limitations and makes it a viable belief for all time.[5]

Schweitzer's analysis of Paul's apocalyptic eschatology has not stood up as well as his work on Jesus. There is considerable agreement that Paul's writings do not contain a messianic interregnum or a second resurrection. The Jewish apocalyptic writings of the time are also much more complex than Schweitzer portrays them to be, for there are many different and often conflicting views of the resurrection, postmortem punishments and rewards, and the afterlife.

Rudolf Bultmann believed that Paul was reinterpreting or demythologizing the apocalyptic tradition that he had received, especially elements such as cosmic powers. Paul was concerned with the faith response of the individual human when confronted with the Gospel. Bultmann read Paul through the lenses of his own existentialist reinterpretation of the New Testament.[6]

According to **Ernst Käsemann,** Paul's apocalyptic eschatology asks the fundamental apocalyptic question: To whom does the sovereignty of the world belong? To God or the evil powers? God has invaded the realm of these powers, and believers are in the midst of a war between these two spheres of power for sovereignty of the world that began with the death and resurrection of Christ. Paul's theology of the resurrection is described in 1 Corinthians 15:20–28, but the focus is christological rather than anthropological, since the important element is the work of the Second Adam and his rule. This rule eventually gives way to the total reign of God, with Christ acting as God's agent in a world not totally subject to God.[7]

Apocalyptic as the Abiding Center of Paul's Gospel

J. Christiaan Beker has been the modern champion of the apocalyptic interpretation of Paul. He defines Paul's gospel as apocalyptic because "it looks forward to the final triumph of God in Christ over all those powers in the world that resist his redemptive purpose." The center of Paul's gospel is the conviction that the death and resurrection of Christ have opened up a new future for the world. The climax of this future is the reign of God, defined as the event that will bring the created order to the fulfillment of its divine destiny.[8]

He finds in Paul's gospel what he considers to be the four basic components of Jewish apocalyptic: vindication, universalism, dualism, and imminence. *Vindication* is reflected in the conviction that the Covenant God of Israel has confirmed and renewed his promises of salvation to Israel and to the nations. *Universalism* represents the cosmic nature of God's majesty and glory. At the end of time, there is a cosmic vindication characterized in part by the radical reversal of all values. *Dualism* is an expression of the powers of evil, which are obstacles to God's plan of salvation. In Jewish apocalyptic, there was a stark contrast between this world and the world to come; when the latter arrives, nature as well as humans will be transformed. *Imminence* characterizes the impending actualization of God's reign. Due to this imminence, all the other motifs are intensified. There is a strong hope for the completion of God's universal dominion and the elimination of dualistic and unjust structures.[9]

Paul has often been accused of inconsistency and contradiction. This is only the case, however, if we impose a modern theological structure on the letters. Rather than viewing Paul's letters as systematic and timeless theological treatises, Beker stresses that they are the embodiment of the coherent center in contingent and historical circumstances.[10]

The coherent center of Paul's gospel is his apocalyptic interpretation of the Christ event.[11] Paul modified traditional apocalyptic thought in three ways: (1) he does not use the usual apocalyptic term "this age" in conjunction with "the age to come"; (2) he modifies the traditional apocalyptic view of the escalation of the forces of evil in the end time; (3) he rarely uses the term "the Kingdom of God" (or "the day of the Lord"), and when he does, it is mainly in traditional contexts.[12]

Beker holds that the apocalyptic motif forms the foundation of Paul's thought and that the apocalyptic triumph of God is its focal point. This core or center Beker prefers to call coherence, allowing more fluidity and flexibility, and is "determined by Paul's apocalyptic interpretation of the Christ-event and culminates in God's triumph over all the powers that are opposed to his rightful lordship over creation."[13] Beker states that the coherence-contingency dialectic is similar to the theory-praxis debate in liberation theology. The question is then raised whether the theological authenticity of praxis is self-generating and whether the authority of scripture hinges on the proper relationship between coherency and contingency.[14]

Resurrection language is apocalyptic end-time language, since it refers not to removal from the world, but refers to the world to come, a restored and renewed world. It expresses the presence of a new age in the midst of the old. This is exemplified in chapter 15 of 1 Corinthians, in which Paul argues that the resurrection of Christ cannot be separated from the future apocalyptic resurrection of the dead. The resurrection of Christ is an event that inaugurates the end of history, and cannot be understood apart from the general resurrection (1 Cor 15:20; Rom 8:29; cf. Col 1:16). Since the Corinthian community was interpreting the Christ event in terms of a Hellenistic cosmic dualism and denigration of the body, Paul must demonstrate that the resurrection of believers is both a future and somatic event.[15] Paul uses the term "hope" often, and this hope is directed toward this future event of the parousia and glory, which is situated in space and time.[16]

There are a number of ways in which Paul's interpretation of the death of Christ is imbedded in an apocalyptic framework. First of all, his death is understood as having stripped apocalyptic forces such as sin, flesh, and the law of their power and signals the imminent overthrow of death. Christ's death represents God's judgment on the old age. Paul intensifies this Jewish apocalyptic motif and also transforms it, in the sense that Christ's death changes both conditions after death and the elitist or exclusivist views of Jewish apocalyptic. Gone are the descriptions of an exulting in the tortures and punishment of the wicked. The death of Christ is inseparably connected with his resurrection, which is the inauguration of the cosmic triumph of God. When this is misinterpreted, both the cross and the resurrection are distorted and easily collapse into a theology of glory or an individualistic theology of the cross. Finally, the death and resurrection of Christ are consecutive events, which reflect its apocalyptic background. This stresses the finality of Christ's death and the destruction of the evil forces, but this finality is incomplete until the consummation of the new age. Whereas Christians have died with Christ, they have not yet been raised. Christ's victory over death is for Christians still in the realm of hope.[17]

Vincent Branick agrees with much of Beker's work, but he balances what he believes to be a "one-sidedness" in Beker's presentation. He focuses on some strong inconsistencies in Paul's use of apocalyptic, which he believes to be characteristic of transitional thinking, and a growing openness on his part to realized eschatology.[18] He wishes, therefore, to challenge Beker's assertion that the "apocalyptic structure of thought" forms the consistent and indispensable center of his thought.

He points to the tension in the "already" and "not yet." God's victory has been won in Christ, but sin and death still exist for believers. The Gospel of John (11:25–26) and the Letter to the Ephesians (2:5–6) solve the problem by fashioning a realized eschatology: The believer already possesses the resurrection and salvation on the spiritual level.

A number of themes present in the Pauline writings are the seeds of a realized eschatology in Paul. Among them are: (1) newness of life (Rom 6:4); (2) interior transformation (2 Cor 4:16); (3) spiritual existence (1 Cor 15; 1 Cor 1:18—2:16); (4) present abundance of such things as grace, gifts, glory, love, hope, and power of the spirit (Rom 5:15; 2 Cor 4:15; 9:8; Rom 15:13; 1 Cor 14:12; 15:58; 2 Cor 1:5; 3:9; 8:7; 1 Thess 3:12; 4:10; Phil 1:9; (5) sharing in Christ (2 Cor 5:17; Rom 6:3–4. All of these are related to Paul's use of the term *koinōnia* or "sharing" to describe the reality between himself and members of his communities. He also speaks of a *koinōnia* in the Eucharist (1 Cor 10:16) and the spirit (2 Cor 13:13), as well as sufferings (Phil 3:10). These elements reflect a participation rather than apocalyptic language-world. This other side of Paul's thought has deeply transformed his apocalyptic views.[19]

The difficulty in the "already" and "not yet" tension in Paul is resolved when the participation language is recognized. The believer lives a life of transformation that is a progressive intensification of "life" (2 Cor 2:16 and 3:18). Any of the "already" statements in Paul are qualified by "in Christ." One can then say that death is at the same time conquered and still the last enemy, for it is only "in Christ" that sin and death are now meaningless. *"To the degree that* a Christian exists 'in Christ,' the same holds true for that Christian. Paul clearly implies that this existence in Christ is partial for the Christian. Presently it involves an inner reality. At the end it will extend fully to the bodily dimensions of our lives." In his willingness to speak in terms of degrees and progressive and partial transformation, Paul provides the key for resolving the paradox of the "already" and "not yet."[20]

Leander Keck, although accepting apocalyptic eschatology in Paul, is considerably more cautious in his approach than Beker and others.[21] In exploring the relationship between Paul and apocalyptic theology, he notes the problem with defining apocalyptic and the propensity for misusing the terminology. He argues that for Paul theodicy is the end point (Rom 9—11) rather than the starting point. Since God saves the ungodly and sinful, there is no longer any need for him to reward the just and punish the wicked. The cross and resurrection of Jesus was God's response to suffering, and the resurrection was the eschatological event launching the end-time sequence of events. He also uses the two-age language: "...two-aeon [age] thinking coheres with his deepest convictions about the meaning of Christ as the God-given alternative to everything that has gone wrong since Adam. Apocalyptic theology's two-aeon thinking allowed Paul to grasp the universality of the problem and its solution, and to see both in a unitary way."[22]

He believes Paul to be more radical than conventional apocalyptic theology, which stresses human free will and the human origins of sin. Citing Galatians 3:23–25; 5:3; 4:10; and 2:4, he notes that Paul believes humanity to be enslaved by "elemental spirits" or "the Law," and that not even 1 Enoch regards humanity as enslaved to the interfering rebellious angels. Here, however, we might draw attention to de Boer's observation that both the forensic and cosmological models of apocalyptic theology are often interwoven in the same documents, and this includes the letters of Paul.[23] He also views sin as a power dwelling within and taking control of human beings. Unlike most apocalyptic literature, Paul does not describe or delight in the punishments and torments of the wicked, nor does he threaten his believers with hell. In Paul there is a great tension between the "already" and the "not yet," which is usually absent in apocalyptic thought. Jewish apocalyptic theology does not have a sudden appearance of a messianic figure who in a previous appearance has already brought about salvation.

Keck's conclusion is that Paul is apocalyptic not because of Beker's vindication, universalism, dualism, and imminence, for these can apply to other theologies, but because of his perspective of discontinuity and disjunction. Paul's *interpretation* of the Christ event is apocalyptic, although he did not produce apocalyptic in his letters, but "his own creative grasp of the consequences of the Christ-event, a grasp which transformed Christian tradition and experience no less than it did apocalyptic—or any other—theology."[24]

Something has gone terribly wrong and needs to be set right. This is the conclusion **J. Louis Martyn** reaches after studying Paul's letters, especially Galatians and Romans. In Romans 1:18–32, Paul rails about the ungodliness of those who by their wickedness suppress the truth. Human beings have been enslaved by powerful forces who wage war against God. There is almost no talk of repentance and forgiveness in Paul's letters—things have gone so far that only a dramatic and powerful intervention by God can correct the situation.[25]

Much of Martyn's study focuses on Galatians, not a letter usually associated with apocalyptic eschatology, a perception that he is quick to correct. The key passage in his analysis is Galatians 6:14b–15, in which Paul says he has been crucified to the cosmos and that there is a new creation; in effect, he is referring to two different worlds. Martyn notes that in Paul's discussion of circumcision, he does not refer to its opposite, but negates both: circumcision and noncircumcision. He is negating an antinomy. An antinomy is a pair of opposites, and in the ancient world they were viewed as the fundamental building blocks of the cosmos. In his negation, Paul is saying that the cosmos has suffered a death, and that a new one is coming into being. The disappearance of old antinomies can only be an apocalyptic event, the prime example being those negated in Galatians 3:27–28: Jew/Greek; slave/free; male/female. Those baptized into Christ have died to the old cosmos by being crucified with him, and the polarity of the old order is replaced by unity in Christ. The advent of the spirit causes new antinomies to appear, especially in the opposing powers of spirit and flesh. The question the believer must ask is: What time is it? And the answer is: It is the dawn of a new creation, which is embodied in Christ, the church, and the Israel of God.[26]

An apocalyptic understanding of Paul can shift our understanding of some of the classic theological ideas, such as justification by faith. Martyn studies two passages, Galatians 2:16–21 and 3:6—4:7, in this light with interesting results. In the first passage, Paul emphasizes the antinomy of Christ's faith, death, and observance of the Law; in the second, the antinomy is illuminated by a cosmic apocalyptic understanding, in which God is rectifying everything by defeating his enemies through the agency of Christ. Humanity is enslaved to sin, and the rectification or justification that God grants to us in Christ is not forgiveness but liberation or freedom. This is accomplished through the faith of Christ, not ours. "God has set things right without laying down a prior condition of any sort. God's rectifying act, that is to say, is no more God's response to human faith in Christ than it is God's response to human observance of the Law. God's rectification is not God's response at all. It is the first move; it is God's initiative, carried out by him in Christ's faithful death."[27] The polemical nature of Paul's doctrine is merely the reflection of God's polemical act in Christ, and the first cannot be minimized without doing the same to the second.

The new age even brings with it a new epistemology or way of knowing. The statement in 2 Corinthians 5:16–17 that in Christ there is a new creation has become a theological and religious cliché. Paul, however, saw himself as standing at the juncture of the ages, facing humanity in one direction and God in the other.[28] There are two ways of knowing, the physical and the spiritual; and the death/resurrection of Christ, which objectifies the turn of the ages, is what separates the two (1 Cor 2:6–16). The norm of the flesh is the mode of knowing that characterizes the old age, but since they are only at the juncture of the ages and not the fullness, the mode of knowing is now not by the spirit but by the cross and the faith that is active in love in the community.

Martinus C. de Boer sees Paul's apocalyptic eschatology most clearly in the parousia passages, in which Paul speaks of *apokalypsis,* or revelation of the Lord (1 Cor 1:7; cf. 2 Thess 1:7; 1 Thess 4:13–18; and 1 Cor 15:20–28, 50–56). The parousia is the finale of a long chain of apocalyptic events.[29]

He distinguishes apocalyptic eschatology from the traditional definition of eschatology; the first he defines as being "fundamentally concerned with God's active and visible rectification (putting right) of the created world (the "cosmos"), which has somehow gone astray and become alienated from God."[30] Traditional prophetic eschatology anticipated a future divine intervention in the continuing history of Israel. The scope of apocalyptic eschatology is cosmic, encompassing all places and human beings. Even as God's rectifying intervention brings an end to history, it reaches back to its very beginnings.[31]

The opening lines of the Book of Revelation refer to the "revelation of Jesus Christ." De Boer indicates that this is a Pauline and Christian modification of the traditional apocalyptic eschatology in that it uses as a point of departure a past event; namely, the resurrection and ascension.[32]

De Boer focuses on the doctrine of the two ages as being constitutive and distinctive of apocalyptic eschatology, He detects two patterns of Jewish apocalyptic eschatology: one cosmological, the other forensic (legal or juridical), in which cosmic or angelic forces do not play a role.[33]

In the cosmic pattern, the created world has come under the control of evil forces. The sovereignty of God has been usurped, and his people, along with the world, have been lured into slavery and idolatry. A faithful and righteous remnant chosen by God bears witness to the eventual defeat of these evil cosmological powers. The remnant, God's elect, waits for deliverance at God's hand. This will occur when he invades the world that is in the thrall of the evil powers and defeats them in a cosmic battle. God then reasserts his rule, delivering the righteous, and ushering in a new age under his unopposed dominion.[34]

In the forensic model, the evil cosmological forces are absent or only in the background, and at times explicitly rejected (cf. 1 Enoch 98:4–5; Psalms of Solomon 9:4–5). The exercise of free will and individual human decision is paramount. Death is punishment for the fundamental sin of rejecting God. God has provided the law as a remedy or means of rescue, and one's destiny is determined by his or her conformity or adherence to the law. The last judgment, instead of being a cosmic war, is a cosmic courtroom with God as the judge. Those who have observed his commandments and acknowledged his sovereign rule will be rewarded with eternal life, while those who have not will be punished with eternal death. The present age is a time of decision. This form of apocalyptic eschatology is characterized by a legal piety that stresses personal responsibility and accountability.[35] In some works, especially the Dead Sea Scrolls, both tracks coexist. Subjection to evil cosmological forces and human free will, God's cosmic war against the forces of evil and divine judgment based upon deeds or works, seem to cohere happily in the same documents.[36]

Both of these two "tracks" are found in the letters of Paul. In 1 Corinthians 15:12–21 (cf. 2 Cor 11:3; 1 Tim 2:13–14) he uses the story of Adam, which reflects the disobedience motif found in 4 Ezra and 2 Baruch. At the same time, he refers to Satan as a power hostile to God and the Gospel of Christ (Rom 16:20; 1 Cor 5:5; 7:5; 2 Cor 2:11; 11:14; 12:7; 1 Thess 2:18; cf. 2 Cor 6:14; 1 Thess 3:5) indicating that the worldview of cosmological Jewish apocalyptic eschatology was very much a part of his own eschatology.[37]

This two-ages dualism also permeates the letter to the Galatians, chiefly in the conflict between flesh and spirit in Galatians 5:16–26. Its purpose in the letter is to proclaim the Gospel, which is Christ's atoning death for our sins, which delivers humans from the "present evil age" (1:4).

How does Paul's apocalyptic worldview affect his theology? In his study, *The Defeat of Death,* de Boer focuses on Paul's apocalyptic view of death. He holds that Paul's "christologically determined apocalyptic eschatology" is evident in his image of death as expressed in 1 Corinthians 15 and Romans 5. Death is associated with the old age, and it defines the relationship of the human world to God, and it is characterized by separateness and exclusion. There are three dimensions to death: physical, moral (sin), and eternal perdition (eschatological death).[38] Death falls within the cosmological apocalyptic stream, and is personified as an "inimical, murderous, quasi-angelic power that has held all Adamic humanity in subjection and enslavement." The death of Christ is God's invasion of this age, which unmasks the nature of sin and death. It is through Christ's death that God is able to establish his sovereignty over the world.[39]

De Boer asks a number of questions that arise in the study of Paul's letters: Did Paul's views concerning the parousia and the resurrection of the dead develop or change? He answers in the negative, for when the deutero-Pauline letters are excised from the analysis, and the occasional nature of the letters—for they were not dogmatic or systematic treatises—are taken into account, the differences found in various letters may just reflect different issues that are being addressed.[40] He also concludes (along with many others) that there is no messianic interregnum between the parousia and the end. This had been an important element in Schweitzer's reconstruction of Paul's theology.

Aspects of Paul's Apocalyptic

Paul's vision in 2 Corinthians 12:1–12 is placed in the context of apocalyptic mysticism. Indeed, **Paul Segal** insists that in the first century, apocalyptic was mystical by nature and that many of the visions recorded in apocalypses are records of genuine experiences. In Galatians 1:2, Paul claimed that his gospel was not received by means of human tradition, but was revealed, which gave his own claims added validity.[41]

The parousia (second coming of Christ) is an essential component of Paul's apocalyptic theology. This is the focus of three Pauline texts, 1 Thessalonians 4:13–18 and 5:1–11; 1 Corinthians 15:23–28 and 50–58; and Philippians 3:20–31. In a detailed exegetical and theological study of these texts, **Joseph Plevnik** argues against Bultmann's view that the apocalyptic elements must be demythologized or even excised. Plevnik's approach is to rephrase the message embedded in these texts in terms that are meaningful to the present age.[42]

Apocalyptic language is used in these texts for specific purposes, and each text uses its own language and symbols, most of which flow from the Jewish apocalyptic tradition. Consistency of thought is not an issue. Paul is affirming three basic realities: God's promise in Christ to raise us to life with him is unaffected by death (1 Thess); Christ will conquer all opposition to God and establish a life without sin, conflict, and death, and will continue his work until his coming, when the Kingdom will arrive and there will no longer be death (1 Cor 15:23–28, 52–55; and we must raise our gaze from earthly realities to a transcendent home that is the completion and fulfillment of our earthly life (Phil 3:20–21).[43]

Paul's Word of the Cross in 1 Corinthians 2:1–5 is presented as an apocalyptic mystery, according to **Alexandra Brown.** Terms such as "mystery of God" and "fear and trembling" she finds express apocalyptic concepts. Through the use of this symbolism and mystical imagery, Paul struggles to bring a new world to consciousness by leading his followers to an experience of the Spirit, which enables one to have the "mind of Christ" (2:16).[44]

This requires a transformation of the human mind by means of the Spirit, for the disposition of one's mind is determinative of relationships with God and others in body, mind, and spirit.[45] The Spirit, which is the mediator of God's mystery, reveals God as the one who saves humankind through self-giving love rather than merit. This understanding changes one's perception so that God, self, and the world are then known according to the cross.[46] The knowledge imparted by the Spirit that one belongs to God sets one to love God and others freely for the first time, transferring one from the world defined by human categories of wisdom and power to the new creation.[47]

Conclusion

Paul inherited an apocalyptic worldview that was very much part of Second Temple Judaism, not merely a fringe movement as previously thought. The ancients were content with paradox and apparent contradiction, and this is no less true for the apocalypticist. Jewish apocalyptic literature is filled with visions and symbols that clash on a superficial level but witness to the same message on a deeper one: the justice of God, vindication of the just, punishment of the wicked, and the re-creation or renewal of the world. This is very much Paul's concern, and he modified this apocalyptic eschatology in light of the Christ event, viewing the resurrection of Jesus as the first stage in the apocalyptic drama that would be complete only at the parousia or second coming.

4
Apocalypse Now

Then I saw an angel coming down from heaven, holding in his hand the key to the bottomless pit and a great chain. He seized the dragon, that ancient serpent, who is the Devil and Satan, and bound him for a thousand years, and threw him into the pit, and locked and sealed it over him, so that he would deceive the nations no more, until the thousand years were ended. After that he must be let out for a little while. Then I saw thrones, and those seated on them were given authority to judge. I also saw the souls of those who had been beheaded for their testimony to Jesus and for the word of God. They had not worshiped the beast or its image and had not received its mark on their foreheads or their hands. They came to life and reigned with Christ a thousand years. (Rev 20:1)

What Did John Know and When Did He Know It?

The millennium described above is a thousand-year period of Christ's earthly reign with the resurrected martyrs. This occurs after the destruction of Satan's power and before the creation of a God-ruled eternal age of justice and peace. When is this millennium of peace and godly reign to take place? Was John describing past events, or was he predicting the future? If he were predicting the future, was he referring to the imminent future or did he have the whole sweep of human history in mind? The interpretation of this passage is a touchstone for determining one's theological stance and methodology. Amillennialists interpret this thousand-year period in a symbolic or allegorical sense to mean the victorious and eternal reign of the saints with Christ. The premillennial view holds that Christ will return prior to that millennial reign, while postmillennialists hold that his return will occur after its completion. Premillennialism is the reigning evangelical theology in North America.[1]

The amount of material on the Book of Revelation is enormous, and has only increased in the years leading up to the new millennium. We will touch on a few representative examples of the different interpretative approaches. It might seem that there are as many different scholarly opinions as there are scholars. In a very helpful introductory essay, **Eugene Boring** places the different approaches to the Book of Revelation into four basic categories or patterns.[2]

The first of these is the nonhistorical approach, characterized by interpretations that are poetic, spiritual, allegorical, or idealistic. The text itself is seen as containing timeless truths. A good example of this approach is **Edward Edinger's** Jungian psychological analysis of Revelation. As a Jungian analyst, Edinger believes that the world as we know it is indeed coming to an end soon. But these events are psychological events, and much of the turmoil and bloodshed in societies over the centuries has been the result of this psychological transition from one cultural era to another. His psychological exegesis of Revelation provides, he believes, the insights we will need to understand the process and to weather the storm. Acts of fanatical terrorism, such as the Oklahoma City bombing, are the results of individuals being "possessed" by the apocalypse archetype, that is, being the heroic figure at war with the forces of darkness.[3]

The second is the church-historical approach, in which the book is viewed as a long-range prediction of future events until the end of time. The book is relevant to each age because the events of each age have been predicted. The problem with this approach, as with some others, is that the book would have been largely incomprehensible to the first generation to which it was addressed. The writings of the medieval mystic Joachim of Fiore fall into this category, because he divided the history of the church into different periods, placing his own time in the final period. During the Reformation, both Catholics and Protestants used Revelation in this manner, painting their opponents in its negative imagery.[4]

The end-time historical approach, a radically futurist viewpoint, is perhaps the most well-known, since this is the stuff of pop eschatology and fundamentalist end-time preachers. Hal Lindsey's famous end-time book *The Late Great Planet Earth* is a prime example.[5] The dispensationalist and premillennialist interpretations of Revelation fall into this group. In a periodized scheme of church history, the last period is considered apostate, and is each interpreter's own time. The predictions in Revelation pertain only to the last few years of world history, and we live in the time just before the final events. All the eschatology is considered as pertaining to the interpreter's own lifetime. In many of these modern interpretations, the fulfillment of the prophecies requires world war and nuclear destruction. Again, the predictions would not have been understood by the recipients of the letter, and the work would have had nothing to say to people living in the intervening periods of history.

The contemporary-historical is sometimes called the preterist (past tense) approach. Revelation is viewed as being written in response to particular first-century conditions, and it is analyzed in that original historical context. The events or conditions alluded to in the document have already taken place. This is the approach utilized by critical scholars of the New Testament. As a general principle, modern interpreters cannot accept any interpretation that its first readers would not have understood.

The Book of Daniel and the New Testament

No discussion of NT apocalyptic literature and the Book of Revelation can exclude the Book of Daniel, for it is the bedrock of both Jewish apocalyptic writings (especially Baruch and Ezra) and the apocalyptic elements of the New Testament. Chapters 7—12 of Daniel have generated most of the New Testament's apocalyptic imagery. Mark 13 (the "little apocalypse"), has been described as an extended midrash or meditation on several Danielic elements: the end, tribulations, the desolating sacrilege, the need for perseverance, and the coming of the Son of Man. Daniel 7 is the formative element in 1 Thessalonians 4:5 and 1 Corinthians 15:23–28. Mark and Luke both begin their Gospels with an announcement that the "time is fulfilled," referring to the promises of Daniel 2:44 and 7:22. The abomination of desolation in 9:27 plays a key role in the little apocalypse of the Synoptic Gospels. In John, Jesus speaks of the resurrection in terms of Daniel 12 (John 5:28–29 as well as Matt 13:43 and 25:46). The depiction of Antioches Epiphanes in Daniel 7–11 is the basis of the Lawless One of 2 Thessalonians 2. The vision of the beasts in Daniel 7 was drawn on for the vision of the new beast, Rome, in Revelation 13 and 17. Finally, chapter 12 stresses the resurrection and exhorts its listeners to endurance in the face of tribulations, dominant themes in Revelation.[6]

With its detailed apocalyptic timetables and rich symbolism, Daniel has fuelled end-time computation from its birth until our own times. The Arab-Israeli war of 1967 was seen by some as being a fulfillment of Daniel 8:14 and 12:12 because it occurred 2,300 years after the conquest of Alexander and 1,335 years after the establishment of the Muslim Caliphate.[7]

In modern scholarship, however, there is a virtual consensus with regard to the dating, genre, purpose, and historical setting of Daniel. Rather than being written in Babylon during the seventh and sixth centuries B.C.E. as the story's setting suggests, it was compiled in the second century B.C.E., during the Maccabean

Revolt, in response to struggle and persecution at the hands of Antioches IV Epiphanes. Daniel is an apocalypse, the only complete example of this genre in the Old Testament. The character of Daniel is probably legendary, and the nature of the work is pseudonymous.[8] Chapters 1–6 appear to be tales of an earlier date, while chapters 7–12 consist of a series of visions. The author appears to have integrated both the tales and visions into the unity of his work, which can be described as an example of historical literary fiction.[9]

The Book of Daniel reflects historical experience and events, but is not historiography and it does not predict the future. Because of persecution of the Jews, there are several attempts to specify the number of days before God's intervention. The reader is left with the conviction that events are predetermined and guided by higher powers, and that the wise are destined for a resurrected life. The book enabled Jews to cope with the crisis of persecution, convinced that evil will eventually be overcome by the sovereign and mighty God of Israel, who hears prayers and grants revelations.[10]

The Quest for the Historical Domitian

When was Revelation written, and was its audience experiencing persecution? The answer to those two questions determines how the text is interpreted. The received wisdom held that the book was composed during the reign of Domitian, around 95 C.E. Domitian had the reputation for tyranny, erratic and cruel behavior, and pretensions to divinity. Revelation was written, it was said, to encourage believers who were experiencing savage persecution at Roman hands and refusing to worship the emperor. All of this has come under question, and the research of **Leonard Thompson** and others has raised the question as to whether Revelation was intended to encourage those under persecution or rouse those who were all too comfortable and accommodating with the status quo. In various forms and degrees, this new view of the reign of Domitian and the purpose for which Revelation was written has achieved wide acceptance in commentaries and studies.

Thompson reappraised the long-accepted view by analyzing the Roman historiography and rhetoric associated with Domitian and his reign, and concludes that the negative depictions of Domitian are not at the hands of neutral observers, but reflect the political and propaganda concerns of subsequent emperors. He also doubts that Domitian insisted on the title *dominus et deus* (Lord and God) or that he was a mad tyrant bent on acquiring divine honors.[11]

These conclusions impact on the interpretation of Revelation. Thompson stresses the wealth, prosperity, and culture of the empire and its cities during this period, and insists that Christians were leading quiet lives, very content to enjoy the benefits offered by the empire. And that is the problem! John is writing to rouse his followers from their complacency and lethargy. He finds their willingness to enjoy the benefits of empire and to have dealings with non-Christians abhorrent. The Roman culture and society are corrupt and evil, and as a religious visionary, John calls them to come out of empire (18:4) and to embrace what is more fundamental and comprehensive, God's Kingdom.[12]

Thompson denies that there is anything dualistic in John's worldview. As God is the creator and sustainer of all things, there is no spatial or temporal dualism between the kingdom of the world and the Kingdom of God. His vision is one of unbroken wholeness, and boundaries of any sort are points of transaction where all elements that are seemingly opposed undergo adjustment and transformation in order to contribute to the coherence and wholeness of existence.[13] This section of his book is not entirely convincing. Apocalyptic was thoroughly dualistic if nothing else, and the complete unity and wholeness is achieved only after the total victory of God, when all opposition has been subjugated or destroyed. Apocalyptic writings are consistent in this outlook.

Thompson is certainly correct in asserting that classical historical texts cannot be taken at face value any more than can biblical texts. A thorough examination of scholarly assumptions is always welcome and salutary. It does seem strange, however, that ancient historians such as Pliny, Tacitus, Suetonius, and Dio Cassius are so united in their extremely negative assessment of Domitian and his reign. Christian sources also reflect the same attitude. Although sources from the time of Domitian's reign are more positive, this is certainly to be expected, for attacking any emperor, especially one with his reputation, would have been suicidal. Thompson states that there is no evidence of a general official persecution of Christians during Domitian's reign. This may be true, but the fact that the persecutions of Domitian's reign are not officially reported should not surprise us at all. Oppressive governments certainly do not label their actions in a negative fashion or draw attention to them. What the victims experience as oppression might appear to be sane social and political policy to those in power. It strains credulity to assume that both the persecution under Domitian's reign and his tyranny and megalomania, both attested in many sources, were contrived.

Adela Yarbro Collins continues in this vein in her challenging and insightful work *Crisis and Catharsis*. Her approach combines the historical-critical method, literary criticism, and psychological insights from socioscientific theory. She too rejects the commonly held idea that there was widespread official persecution during this period or that Domitian tried to impose the cult of the emperor's divinity on his subjects.[14] The work was written by John to draw attention to a crisis not perceived by many Christians.[15]

According to Collins, John wrote Revelation because of a conflict between his view of the Christian faith and the social situation as he saw it. New expectations were created by Jesus as the Messiah, and by the Kingdom of God and Christ. John was prompted to write Revelation because of the tension between this and his environment. The crisis and trauma that he experienced were on a social level, involving rejection, suspicion, and repression on the part of outsiders. John's response was to call the Christian community to a life of social radicalism.[16]

Through the use of violent and bellicose imagery and language, his visions are meant to absolutely demonize Rome and to reinforce anti-Roman feelings already present in the listeners, or provoke such an attitude in those who were ambivalent or even accepting of Roman culture. This is especially true in chapters 17 and 18, where Rome is labeled the new Babylon and the mother of harlots and its eventual demise foretold. Rome is denounced for arrogance, violence, self-glorification, wealth, blasphemy, and oppression. John, in Collins's view, was an itinerant prophet who preached social radicalism in the form of nonparticipation in Greco-Roman society, detachment from wealth and property, continence, exclusivity, and expectation of an imminent judgment against their enemies.[17]

Through its symbols and artistry, Revelation clarified, simplified, and brought to awareness feelings that had probably been vague, latent, complex, and ambiguous. This approach is very dualistic, since Jews and those who lacked God's seal, thereby belonging to the beast, are doomed to destruction. Collins believes that through the symbols, fear and aggressive feelings were heightened, then projected onto a cosmic screen. This led to catharsis and the ability to be detached from feelings and to gain self-control. This was in some sense inadequate, for rigorism and superhuman standards were eventually transformed into new kinds of aggressive feelings.[18]

She is very critical of Revelation and what she perceives to be its failure in love and its disregard for human values. This is most fully expressed in the division of humanity into two camps, those belonging to God and those to the Beast. There is a thread of intolerance and vengeance throughout the work. The imagery is harsh and violent; Christ is portrayed as the divine warrior. She favors a critical reading of Revelation, one in which authority is conferred, not assumed. Approaching the document not to seek information but for its effect on us, can be helpful in illuminating our own negative feelings and aggressive impulses so that we can deal with them. It can also unmask the unjust or demonic inherent in many human institutions that seek power at the expense of others, and impel us to seek to deal with the situation. It must be used with great care, and not in a way that would divide and demonize.[19]

The Jailhouse Perspective

Elisabeth Schüssler-Fiorenza disagrees with many of the points raised by Collins. First of all, she does not accept that Revelation is more about judgment and vengeance than love. She sees Revelation as being in continuity with Jewish apocalyptic but expressing a newness in the experience of Jesus as the resurrected Christ actively present in the Christian community and speaking to it through prophets and apostles. Traditionally, Revelation had been seen as a work more Jewish than Christian, and therefore of little use for the reconstruction of life and theology in the early church. The Christian theological significance had to be distilled from the crude apocalyptic imagery. Today, however, Revelation is seen as a Christian work of a special sort and in its own right.[20]

She also rejects the notion that there was no persecution or crisis, and relying on solid evidence such as the famous letter of Pliny the Younger, she comes to the conclusion that, "John views Roman power as exploitive, destructive, and dehumanizing because he and some of the Asian communities have experienced poverty, banishment, violence and harassment, and assassination."[21]

Babylon/Rome is not the symbol of the "archetypal enmity" against God or of "the decadence of all civilization," but symbolizes imperial power and cult. In Revelation it is the "powerful incarnation of international exploitation, oppression, and murder. Babylon/Rome is intoxicated not only with the blood of the saints but with that of all those slaughtered on earth. Rome's ruthless power and exploitive wealth are enormous and its decrees are carried out in the provinces that support Roman oppression." Revelation 15:5—19:10 becomes, then, a trial in which Babylon/Rome is the defendant, the oppressed and murdered Christians the plaintiffs, and God the judge. God passes judgment against Babylon/Rome, and the heavenly court rejoices along with Christians everywhere.[22]

She parts company with those who see the symbols of Revelation as steno-symbols (Perrin) having exact historical counterparts or who want to extract or distil the theological essence from apocalyptic language. These are tensive symbols, evoking many meanings, and she sees the indeterminacy of the text in positive rather than negative terms.[23]

Schüssler-Fiorenza sees Revelation as a work of visionary rhetoric; that is, it seeks to motivate or persuade people to act right. Its poetic nature invites imaginative participation, while the rhetoric provokes change of attitudes and motivations. Intertwined, these elements strive to construct a symbolic universe that invites imaginative participation. This visionary rhetoric does not draw its persuasive power from theological reasoning or historical arguments. The power instead comes from the evocative power of its symbols as well as in "its hortatory, imaginative, emotional language, and dramatic movement," all of which elicit reactions, emotions, convictions, and identifications from the readers or listeners. For instance, in the account in 14:1–5, visions and auditions of salvations are juxtaposed with those of antidivine powers in order that the hearer be led to make a proper decision for salvation and for God in the face of destructive power represented by the beast, Babylon, and Rome.[24]

To those who criticize Revelation as being heavy on revenge and vengeance and light on the love of the Sermon on the Mount, she replies that it is a work with a "jailhouse perspective, and will be understood only by those who hunger and thirst for righteousness."[25]

David Aune's three-volume commentary is an exhaustive and detailed analysis of every aspect of the Book of Revelation. His historical approach is supplemented with analyses of the text, vocabulary, and structure of the book. The intriguing aspect of his work is the manner in which he handles the seemingly contradictory evidence regarding the date of composition. He notes that the internal and external evidence at times clash; some of the internal evidence favors a composition date of 68–69 C.E. (under Nero), while other evidence seems more compatible with the traditional date of approximately 95 C.E., the period of Domitian's reign. Starting from the increasingly accepted view that there was no general persecution or increased insistence on the imperial cult during Domitian's reign, Aune concludes that it is not necessary to insist on dating the book to this period.[26]

Aune proposes that Revelation is a work that underwent stages of composition. It is a composite work consisting of a series of relatively independent, self-contained, apocalyptic elements that were composed for a wide range of purposes and situations. They were finally revised and formed into a unified literary work. The primitive stages of this work could have begun as early as the 60s and reached completion in the mid-90s. This would explain both the conflicting evidence regarding dating and the presence of both distinctively Jewish and Christian elements. Aune proposes two distinct editions. The first edition includes 1:7–12a and 4:1—22:5. This edition contains the most distinctively apocalyptic material. The title in 1:1–3, the epistolary doxology in 1:4–6, the circular letter to the seven churches in 1:12b—3:22, and the epilogue and epistolary conclusion in 22:6–21 comprise the second edition.[27]

Aune's work has been criticized as representing the rigorously historical approach that is now being challenged, an approach characterized by the assumption that historical events and circumstances generated the text. This leads to an intense focus on a wide range of external ancient sources and parallels to illuminate the meaning of the text. The result is a mound of data that can be helpful in analyzing individual passages but often leaves the reader grappling with how to grasp the "big picture" and how to apply the text to our own time.

Several authors have grounded their work in historical criticism but modified this view with either an idealistic or future-oriented approach. **G. K. Beale's** massive commentary provides a wealth of information and discussion. After surveying the different avenues of approach to Revelation, Beale opts for what he calls an eclectic or redemptive-historical form of modified idealism. Although Revelation prophesies a final consummation in salvation and judgment, no specific historical event is prophesied in the book. Transtemporal symbols are used to portray historical events occurring in the "church age," which lasts until the second coming of Jesus. As transtemporal symbols, however, they may be used to portray events throughout that age.[28]

Beale's research has centered on the OT background of the Book of Revelation, and he insists that it is against this background that we must interpret the images and ideas of the book. Although Greco-Roman sources are also important, the Old Testament provides the primary key for interpretation.[29] The purpose of the symbols is first of all to reveal the transcendent new creation that has begun to penetrate the old order. This has been accomplished through the life, death, and resurrection of Jesus and the sending of the Holy Spirit. The symbols also encourage and exhort its audience to live in harmony of thought and deed with the standards of the new creation. This new creation is the true home of the believer, and the symbols help to ground him or her in that new reality.[30]

The purpose of the work, which Beale describes as "prophecy cast in an apocalyptic mould and written down in letter form,"[31] is "to encourage those not compromising with idolatry to continue in that stance and to jolt those who are compromising out of their spiritual anesthesia so that they will perceive the spiritual danger they are in and repent and become witnesses to the risen Christ as Lord. For those who never respond, only judgment will ensue".[32]

John repeatedly alludes to five OT promises that form a typological interpretation of history: new covenant, new temple, new Israel, new Jerusalem, and new creation. These biblical ideas are metaphors for "the one reality of God's intimate, glorious presence with his people," and their confluence in 21:1—22:5

comprise the climax and dominant message of the book up to that point: God's glorious presence. It is the vision of this unending communion with God's glorious presence that forms the basis of the exhortation to remain faithful.[33]

Catherine Gonzalez and **Justo Gonzalez** draw on the best insights of historical criticism in their short commentary aimed at lay bible study groups. Rather than persecution, they view the main challenge faced by Revelation's first readers as the struggle against an idolatrous and unjust culture and society. John is calling upon his followers to remain faithful to their spiritual ideals and resist the blandishments of their surrounding culture. The authors call for a reading of Revelation that is both historical and futuristic. The historical analysis tells us what John was saying to his readers in the first century. The futurist approach, rather than trying to predict future events, sees that God's future purpose for creation was begun and is guaranteed by the life, death, and resurrection of Christ.[34]

Richard Bauckham focuses on the theology of the Book of Revelation. He views it as an apocalyptic prophecy in the form of a circular letter and the climax of tradition in that it is the fulfillment of OT prophecy. Not only does the reader receive a transcendent perception of the world, but the prophetic aspects of the work confront the reader's historical situation. The book is a carefully crafted blend of evocative images and OT allusions that draw the reader into its symbolic world, and it "creates a reservoir of meaning which can be progressively tapped."[35]

Confronted with Roman oppression and domination, Revelation answers the fundamental question: Who is Lord of the world? The result is a final vision of God's ultimate plan for the world and human history, which expands the spatial and temporal world of his readers.[36]

Revelation's symbols are contextual and not timeless, and an understanding of their relationship with the social, political, and cultural world of the seven churches is crucial for our understanding and appropriation. Symbols such as the seven trumpets (8:6—9:21) and the seven bowls (16:1–21) are evocative of the OT images of the plagues of Egypt, the fall of Jericho, the army of locusts from the Book of Joel, the Sinai theophany, the fear of invasion by Parthian cavalry, and the recent Vesuvius eruption and earthquake. John takes some of the worst and most frightening of contemporary experiences, then casts them in apocalyptic proportions and biblically allusive terms. The purpose of this is not to predict the future, but to disclose the divine judgment that is imminent.[37]

Interestingly, Bauckham rejects the common assumption that Revelation was written to console those suffering persecution. Although that element is present, it serves as more of a call to arms. Many of the hearers are chastised and called to repent.[38]

Novel Approaches

Bruce Malina and **John Pilch** are both well known for their ground-breaking work on the utilization of the tools of the social sciences for the interpretation of the New Testament. In their *Social-Science Commentary on the Book of Revelation,* the authors offer a novel approach to the text, that of ancient astrology. They see John as an astral prophet, and they point out that nearly all the visions in Revelation are related to the sky. In the ancient world, the stars were thought to be celestial entities with souls and intelligence, and people turned to them for the disclosure of hidden secrets. This is also found in Philo's account of Moses and in the Enochic literature.[39]

The authors believe that John was in an altered state of consciousness (ASC) and therefore perceiving alternate realities. These ASCs were common to ancient peoples as they are to some modern people, but since our awareness and perceptions are culturally conditioned, we are formed or programmed by modern Western cultures not to have them and to deny that they exist. He was interpreting the heavens based on both Hellenistic astrological lore and Second Temple Israelite traditions.

The work contains no clear and unambiguous references to either Rome or its emperors, and parts of it probably predate 70 C.E., since it is a composite work.[40] It provides information about the exalted Jesus and his importance for Christians in enabling them to live lives that are peaceful and free of deception.[41] The ancient social system, which included the sky, is encoded in its symbolism. The past is disclosed as the key to understanding the present situation, and future events are prophesied. This book is intended as a supplement to the standard commentaries, and it offers a perspective rarely seen in modern studies of Revelation. Because of modern biases, the relevance of celestial prophecy (astrology) for the ancients, including Israel, is undervalued.

A Distant Mirror

A number of works see the events depicted in Revelation as a distant reflection of our own times and situation. They draw on contemporary scholarship and are historical in their approach, but in a sort of modified idealistic mode, seeking to find the analogue to the first-century situation in our own time. In this approach, Revelation provides us with a means of illuminating our own situation and making appropriate ethical and spiritual choices.

Wes Howard-Brook and **Anthony Gwyther's** provocative work *Unveiling Empire* seeks to reappropriate the message of Revelation for application to modern political and economic situations.

Utilizing both the historical-critical and literary methods of analysis, they situate Revelation in its social and historical context. For John, the crisis was the complacency about empire among his followers. His letter was intended to incite them to resist assimilation into the dominant Roman imperial culture and mindset, which was seen to be characterized by exploitation, violence, arrogance, and pride. They side with those who see no enforcement of the imperial cult under Domitian and only sporadic, local persecution.[42]

Babylon and New Jerusalem are seen as coexistent but contrary realities, and they constitute the master metaphor of the book. John experiences the lifting of the veil of imperial propaganda and sees the pretensions of Rome for what they are and that the empire is really Babylon. Babylon exists wherever sociopolitical power forms an entity that encroaches on the worship that is God's alone, and symbolizes God's judgment on all human attempts to substitute these forms of power for God. The New Jerusalem, on the other hand, "is found wherever the human community rejects the lies and violence of empire and places God at the center of its shared life."[43]

Choices must be made, and there is the dramatic imperative in 18:4 to "Come out!!" In a modern setting this means to resist and withdraw from economic, social, political, and spiritual compromises and to create alternatives. The usual suspects are rounded up: globalization, NAFTA, GATT, economic exploitation, environmental issues, militarism, and the U.S. They suggest practical ways of nonparticipation, that is, "coming out" of empire in the form of alternative lifestyles and economics.[44]

In his article "Reading Revelation Today: Witness as Active Resistance," **Brian Blount** maintains that texts as well as words are polyvalent, and meaning is dependent on context. The poetic and apocalyptic language of Revelation was understood to be the language of nonviolent resistance, and in his analysis of several passages, especially 12:1–17, he finds a witness to active resistance as well as cultic, social, and political transformation. Interpreting Revelation in the context of the American civil rights struggle, he sees Martin Luther King as responding to John's call for active but nonviolent resistance.[45]

In their painstaking examination of the minutiae and structure of Revelation, scholars often overlook the fact that this work is a narrative or story. In his commentary *Tales of the End,* **David Barr** proposes that Revelation is a story about Jesus. He prescinds from most of the usual political, theological, and academic concerns in his literary analysis, concentrating instead on the sonic and visual symbolism as well as the structure and plot.[46]

He discerns three distinct and interrelated movements in a common frame: John on Patmos (1—3), which is a theophany; the heavenly court, where the Lamb reveals the secrets of the scroll (4—11), in the form of a throne vision; and the cosmic battle with Jesus as the cosmic warrior (12—22), which is portrayed as a holy war. He refers to them as the letter scroll, the worship scroll, and the war scroll respectively. These three dramatic stories are not sequential, but three interrelated narrations of the same Jesus story.[47] John uses the genre of the war story to describe the coming of God's universal dominion in the life and death of Jesus, who has waged a victorious battle with evil and is now able to instruct the churches.[48] The command to worship God is a repeated theme in the story, and the scrolls constantly call the listener to decision and action. The audience is called to persistent resistance and the true worship of God. The worship scroll is liturgical in nature, and the audience of Revelation is comprised of listeners rather than readers. The function of the worship component is to bind them together as a community of shared vision, an army ready to do battle with the cosmic forces of evil. The story of Jesus in the narrative is also the story of each individual.[49]

Barr views all texts as subject to multiple and ongoing interpretations. No one interpretative is definitive or exhaustive, and he gives authority to both the reader and the text in his entreaty at the end of the book, "Hearing the Book of Revelation was an experience meant to transform the listener. Learn to listen." He hopes to provide the literary and culture tools to make this possible.[50]

Conclusion

The Book of Revelation is and has always been a puzzling and opaque book, and any facile assumption about its origin, meaning, or purpose is sure to be incomplete or off the mark. Much will remain closed to us, because we do not share the worldview or religious sensibilities of its author. The book will not only continue to inspire the hearts and minds of believers in one way or another until the end of time, but also provide material for scholars for some time to come. Research has given us, however, some sound principles to apply when interpreting the book. First of all, it must have been intelligible to its first-century audience. It was not written primarily with our own time in mind. It was in the tradition of Jewish apocalyptic, modified by Christian reflection on the death and resurrection of Jesus. It was meant to appeal to the imagination and consciousness, but that does not preclude an expectation on the part of its initial audience of a literal unfolding of many of the events alluded to. Finally, any attempt to appropriate it for our own time, and appropriate it we should, must respect the integrity and meaning of the book in its original context, and not merely as a convenient tool or weapon for our own issues.

5
Apocalyptic, the World, and the Church

"New Age" Preaching

Outside of churches that follow a millennialist or premillennialist interpretation of NT apocalyptic, one seldom hears a homily or sermon on these texts. Many of the clergy simply do not know what to do with them, and to preach in any meaningful way is a challenge. The challenge is not only the level of meaning, but also content and style. Many passages in the Book of Revelation are incredibly violent and hateful in attitude. Other passages encourage misogyny. This challenge is met in a positive and inspiring manner by **David Jacobsen,** in his book *Preaching in the New Creation.* He believes that apocalyptic texts have something to offer the church, and that it is especially important that they be preached in a sound manner in view of their misuse by fearmongers.[1]

Although valuing the results of historical criticism, he prescinds from its effort to "get at the world behind the text," concentrating instead on the ways that the text can alter the world of its hearers. These texts succeed in robbing the established social order of its legitimacy and power. Additionally, the reinterpreted symbolic universe of the incipient new order is presented. In order to do this, the preacher must not just look at what the words say, but at what they are trying to do. The method Jacobsen uses is that of rhetorical analysis, and he offers preachers step-by-step instructions on its application. This is done in conjunction with a comparison of the selected text with similar passages from Jewish apocalyptic writings. He applies this to several texts from Mark 13 and the Book of Revelation, with advice on avoiding pitfalls in the presentation, and an appendix even provides sample homilies.[2]

Apocalyptic and Ethics

One of the criticisms often leveled at apocalyptic theology is that it encourages withdrawal from the world and nonparticipation in its development and healing. In his discussion of the importance of a thorough understanding of the apocalyptic nature of Paul's gospel, Beker insists that this need not be: "...apocalyptic hope completes ethical seriousness, because it is existentially impossible to believe in God's coming triumph and to claim his Holy Spirit without a life style that conforms to that faith....God's triumph will not take place without the participation of our 'neighbors' in it, and so our 'neighbors' compel us to struggle together with them for the liberation of all of God's world."[3] Beker looks to Paul's cosmic anthropology as instrumental in overcoming a division or separation between the personal and social aspects of the gospel.

History has been full of false prophets and false apocalypticism. Beker insists that a truly Pauline apocalyptic gospel will resist these false emissaries and their power because we are motivated by a different apocalyptic vision, that of the theophany of the God of Jesus Christ. Not only is it permissible, but required, that we "live the gospel in such a way that we can be radically open to the concrete demands of our fellow creatures and to the moral issues of our world." Our acts of compassion are incomplete and partial expressions and instruments of God's universal design. Rather than otherworldliness, "the passion for God's kingdom goes hand in hand with our compassion for our needy world."[4]

The delay of the parousia should not disappoint or discourage us; on the contrary, it should serve as a motivation and a sort of "holy aggravation," inspiring both a "sacred impatience" and a patient endurance. The time between the cross and the end-time, regardless of its length, is a time for commitment, decision, mission, and endurance.[5]

Rather than thinking of itself as containing those who are saved, the church should be seen as the "avant-garde of the new creation in a hostile world, creating beachheads in this world of God's dawning new world and yearning for the day of God's visible lordship over his creation, the general resurrection of the dead." It is not possible, however, to transfer Paul's apocalyptic gospel directly into our own time. The only role it can play for us is a catalytic one.[6]

The loss of an understanding of Paul's apocalyptic had tremendous consequences on Christian thought, among them alienation from its Jewish matrix and a spiritualizing of gospel interpretation. The same would also apply for other apocalyptic portions of the New Testament. At the heart of Paul's anthropology was the interrelationship of humanity and the created order. A loss of this understanding contributed to the development of a dualistic anthropology, an increase in asceticism, and a lack of human wholeness. Aiming at both Protestant and Catholic distortions of Paul's gospel, Beker states that "redemption became individual bliss" and the church a "dispenser of sacraments," and the goal was "immortal heavenly status after death" instead of a more communal character. Ethics ultimately was motivated almost entirely from "God's past saving act in Christ" to the detriment of the "compelling and beckoning power of God's final theophany."[7] This is in harmony with the more communal and earthly concept of salvation present in Jewish apocalyptic, as well as the cosmic scope of its vision.

Elisabeth Schüssler-Fiorenza recognizes the combination of apocalyptic patterns and motifs in early Christianity with parenesis, or moral exhortation. She insists that apocalyptic cannot be seen as merely a vehicle for theological or eschatological ideas, but as mythopoetic language that evokes imaginative participation. Since apocalyptic language is metaphorical and symbolic in nature, logical reduction or superficial, one-dimensional interpretation is out of the question. It appeals to the imagination and elicits emotions, insights, and responses that are beyond expression in propositional language.[8]

Most important for Schüssler-Fiorenza's analysis is her appreciation of the New Testament apocalyptic works as religious proclamations that "provoke as a religious narrative, audience participation and catharsis." The apocalyptic narrative carries the readers forward into the future and confirms the hope for their future vindication by God. The function, then, of early Christian apocalyptic is to serve as the creative center of Christian theology, creating a new historical situation and symbolic universe. Prophetic in nature, it proclaims that the Lord Jesus who spoke in the past and will return soon as the eschatological judge is now alive and active in the community.[9]

Walter Wink presents probably the most practical and visionary application of an apocalyptic understanding of the New Testament. Wink's work is born of his participation in the civil rights struggle and antiapartheid campaigns in South Africa. His latest work, *The Powers That Be,* is a condensation of his award-winning trilogy.[10] He takes very seriously the struggle against powers, dominations, and principalities that is indicated in the New Testament, especially in Colossians 1:15–20 and 1 Corinthians 15. In modern usage, they form what Wink calls the Domination System, which rules every aspect of human life, whether economic, social, political, or religious. The structures, systems, and institutions that form the system all have a corresponding corporate personality that is greater than the sum of their parts and is formed by their values, ideals, and deeds. Collectively, they form what he calls "The Powers." Jesus exposed this system, and instead of offering reform or even revolution, he envisioned a "world transformed, where both people and Powers are in harmony with the Ultimate and committed to the general welfare—what some people prefer to call the Kingdom of God.[11] Wink rejects what he calls the myth of redemptive violence in all forms and offers what he calls practical nonviolence for resistance, which he distinguishes from pacifism.[12]

Allan Boesak also writes from the South African struggle with apartheid and his experience of "comfort and protest" while in prison.[13] Apocalyptic literature was concerned with the overthrow of an evil order and tyrants who usurp God's role, as well as the establishment of a just world. This is true of the Book of Revelation.[14] He finds the three approaches to interpreting Revelation inadequate, so he proposes a fourth: contemporary-historical understanding. Rejecting escapist or spiritualized interpretations, he affirms its political message. That which was true in the time of John is an ever-recurring event in the life of the church, which is closely bound with that of the world.[15] His commentary on Revelation is written from the perspective of the suffering and persecuted black people of South Africa, and is intended as both a comfort and a protest.

Pablo Richard takes this even further in his liberationist approach to the Book of Revelation, which he insists is intended to transmit a spirituality of resistance and a vision of an alternative world. The political utopia portrayed in this liberating book is concrete and historical. In its original context, its role was to critique authoritarian and patriarchal structures and institutions, and the church's disregard of this intent permitted it to be compromised and co-opted by the very elements it was supposed to critique. Richard feels that retrieval of this aspect is important not only for transforming the world, but also the church.[16]

His views of eschatology are challenging, for he sees Revelation's eschatology as occurring in the present, rather than anticipating the parousia or the end of the world. With echoes of Bultmann's existentialism, he views the present moment as a graced time of conversion, resistance, witness, and the building of the Kingdom of God. The earthly and the transcendent are merely two dimensions of a unitary history, and they both unfold simultaneously. The hoped-for utopia is not beyond history, but beyond oppression and death in a new world. Myths and symbols grant identity to the community and spur it to action in times of chaos or oppression. Myth also helps to build the "collective consciousness and the social praxis of the people of God," as well as subverting dominant myths and creating ones that are liberating. The Book of Revelation contains the tools and criteria for discerning history from a prophetic stance.[17]

Who Are the Saved? Elitism and Apocalyptic

Apocalyptic movements or churches with a strong apocalyptic eschatology are forever in danger of succumbing to sectarians and elitism. At its "best," this is expressed as an "us-them" mentality. We are the saved. At its very worst, we find the nightmares of Waco, Jonestown, and the Heaven's Gate cult. The elite must retreat from all contact with a tainted, unredeemed society and often resort to provoking or inducing the tribulations or catastrophes that have been so vehemently prophesied. Apocalyptic carries the seeds of this mentality within it; it is found among the Essenes at Qumran and many of the millenarian movements of the early church such as the Montanists. Most recent studies focus on Paul's soteriological views, because his letters predate the Gospels and he had the most to say about the parousia. The issues are whether it is possible for a believer to be denied salvation at the parousia and whether unbelievers are saved or condemned.

J. C. Beker observes that with the nature of apocalyptic itself, properly understood, "there can be no favorite nation clause or claim to privilege before the apocalyptic judgment of God in the cross of Christ.[18]

Others have also dealt with the vexing nature of Paul's views on salvation in an apocalyptic context. Paul is notorious for contradictions and inconsistencies. These are due, no doubt, to the occasional and fluid nature of his letter writing, and it is anachronistic to expect a systematic philosophy from his pen. In the passages relevant to salvation, ambiguity reigns. Some imply exclusive salvation for believers, others universal.[19]

C. H. Dodd tried to show that the "early Paul" taught an apocalyptic "day of wrath" eschatology, which later evolved into a theology of universal salvation found in Romans, Colossians, and Ephesians. His views have not endured, however, due partly to the fact that the latter two epistles are not Pauline, and other studies have shown that there is no clear and definitive linear development in Paul's salvation eschatology.[20] Beker has grappled with this problem from the apocalyptic point of view. The deeper structure or coherent core of Paul's theology, says Beker, is the apocalyptic victory of God. The surface structure can be expressed in symbols that cannot be reconciled on that level, making them seem vague and contradictory. In a sense, he denies that these inconsistencies can or should be reconciled. Paul's thought, however, is corporate and universalist. His arguments are always occasional and contextual, sometimes stressing the universal reign of grace, other times the conditions of participation. Beker's most important observations concerning universal salvation is his statement that "the final apocalyptic triumph of God does not permit a permanent pocket of evil or resistance to God in his creation...everything that opposes God will be overcome or taken up in God's glory."[21] One could just as easily say, however, that opposition to God will be destroyed, and this would be more in keeping with traditional Jewish apocalyptic.

E. P. Sanders believes that in Paul's theology only Christians will be saved. Salvation is achieved by participation in the new reality created by the coming of Christ. Sanders calls this "participationist eschatology," to distinguish it from "covenantal nomism," characterizing the Palestinian Judaism of the time. For Paul, one must convert or transfer from the old reality to the new by faith and commitment, for one cannot be born into this new reality. At the parousia, those in the new reality will be saved, while those of the old will simply be destroyed.[22]

M. Eugene Boring's own study argues the thesis that "the range of Paul's soteriological language—that is, how inclusive it is—is not determined by propositional systematic consistency, nor by his developments in his theology, nor by the tension between depth and surface structures, but by the demands of the central encompassing images within which his language functions, images that necessarily involve him in conflicting language games."[23] A careful analysis of Paul's soteriological language leads Boring to conclude that both the limited and universal salvation passages are valid and need to be taken seriously, and that Paul "be allowed to operate with more than one encompassing image without it being considered a defect, without have to judge Paul incoherent."[24] How is this possible? As statements they cannot be reconciled, nor can one be subordinated to the other, but they must be seen as being generated by the presence of more than one encompassing image. The universalist statements are expressions of the God-the-king image, whose de jure gracious reign is now extended de facto to all of creation. The limited or particularistic statements express the God-as-judge image and the constitutive element of human responsibility. Paul therefore affirms both limited and universal salvation, which affirms both human responsibility and the universal victory of God's grace. Because they are both affirmed together, we are not trapped by the ultimate logical conclusions of each image, and God's grace and judgment can be proclaimed in a manner that cannot be captured in a single system or picture.[25]

Martinus de Boer responds to Boring's study in his 1998 treatment of Paul's apocalyptic. He recognizes, as does Boring, the presence of many soteriological statements that stress human responsibility, and following the lines previously established in his studies, de Boer assigns these to the forensic track of apocalyptic eschatology. Concerning the question of whether sinful Christians can forfeit salvation, de Boer states that although one's salvation in the present can be under threat and that all are cautioned against presumption, in the long term it is doubtful. Salvation is not a human achievement, and to bolster his argument, he appeals to Paul's order that the sinful man in 1 Corinthians 5:1–10 be expelled to the realm of Satan so that he might be saved on the day of the Lord. There are two rich passages that indicate universal salvation: 1 Corinthians 15:21–22 and Romans 5:12–21. Both of these passages parallel on the one hand the universality of Adam's sin, resulting in death, and Christ's action, on the other hand, resulting in life for all. Many scholars have denied Paul really meant that, and have implied that he was trapped by the logic of his own argument. De Boer raises an objection: How can Christ's work be less effective, less cosmic, than Adam's transgression? The whole point of contrasting Adam and Christ is to show that Christ has matched or exceeded the cosmic effects of Adam's sin. De Boer does not come to hard and fast conclusions, and he is aware that Paul's universalist assertions are a stumbling block for many, but he indicates that for Paul faith—upon which salvation depends—always involved "the trustful acknowledgement that salvation is (has been and will be) unconditionally given by God to the ungodly; that is, it is God who effects and thus freely grants salvation....faith is the result of God's prior saving act (the death and resurrection of Jesus), not the condition for it."[26]

Conclusion

The failure of apocalyptic to nourish and invigorate the church is due to our misunderstanding of its true nature and purpose. A lack of hermeneutical imagination hinders our ability to make apocalyptic writings live again in the Christian community in a way that gives hope and contributes to the well-being of humanity. Regardless whether one agrees in entirety with the liberationist approach to apocalyptic, it is clear that they are on the right track in proclaiming that as God spoke to the original first-century audience, so God speaks to every generation in their respective situations. It is not a matter of eternal immutable truths, but of the unity of all human history and the recurring nature of the struggle between those forces aligned with God and those possessed by the quest for power and domination.

Apocalyptic offers a unified vision of creation and of human history. Redemption is seen as encompassing the created order as well as humanity, which offers a hopeful avenue for theological reflection on environmental issues.

The gospel writings are about human life and its struggles in light of the Christ event, and every attempt to remove these apocalyptic writings from the realm of everyday living and the struggle for a just world must be viewed with suspicion. Great care must be taken, however, not to use apocalyptic as a means of inciting people to violence, fanaticism, or intolerance, for this is certainly the dark side of apocalyptic.

6
Conclusion

Interpretation of scripture is never a neutral or inconsequential matter, and one's interpretative model can impact on society and the world. This is especially true of apocalyptic. Several of the books touched on in this study contain sections that give a brief history of apocalyptic and millenarian movements. Nearly every century has had its share of such movements, and they range from the relatively benign to the disastrous. They have all based their interpretation on the assumption that the text was speaking explicitly of their own time; the people of each of these generations saw themselves as living in the "last days," but "the end" seemed to retreat into the distance like a mirage. Both Allison and Ehrman devote portions of their works to a survey of apocalyptic and millenarian movements.

There is certainly a shadowy and sinister side to apocalyptic, or should we say pseudo-apocalyptic. In a sense, these movements are trying to live vicariously the spiritual experience of another generation of long ago. We no longer live in a world that shares the symbolism or cosmological suppositions of the writers of Revelation and other such works. When we no longer share the worldview or understanding of the writers, our own application is bound to be distorted and indicative of our own needs and fears.

Fear represents a major distortion. As we have seen, the literature was intended as a source of hope and courage. Weary and discouraged souls were assured that God was not indifferent to their plight and that the demands of justice and fidelity were not mocked. They were given a vision of something worth struggling, suffering, and even dying for, that is, God's cause. Believers looked beyond the chaotic period of the end to the vision of a new world, one that reflected God's justice rather than human selfishness or indifference.

It is fairly clear that much of the apocalyptic eschatology in the New Testament expected the events portrayed in its symbolism to occur very soon. This was to take the form of the return of Jesus, the resurrection, and the renewal of the world. It was not intended to portray events thousands of years in the future, and the survey of historical apocalyptic movements—sometimes amusing, sometimes poignant—should warn us against the error of self-importance in presuming that we necessarily live in the most important and final period of world history.

At the same time, there is a sense of urgency in the New Testament that cannot be denied or explained away. When this element is lost or denied, a vital aspect of the gospel is missing. This missing element is a vision of God's future for the world and humanity, a dream of the way things could be. If apocalyptic is to be reappropriated for our time, it must not be allowed to be misused as an inducement to fear or indifference to the needs of the planet. We do not know when the return of Jesus will occur. In a sense, it does not matter, for the apocalyptic call to arms enlists us in the quest for a just and compassionate world.

The second distortion is sectarianism and exclusivism, and indeed there are some passages in the Book of Revelation that can support such a view. Apocalyptic movements by nature view themselves as an embattled elite surrounded and besieged by the forces of darkness. One is either with God or against God, in the group of the elect or outside. Here we can appeal to the apocalyptic vision itself, which is universal and cosmic. God's redemptive act in Jesus Christ restores humanity and the entire created order, and we move toward the end of history not aimlessly, but with the renewing and transforming divine energies within us. From our position in history, we have the benefit not only of the quantum leaps in technological sophistication (not to be confused with wisdom!), but the advantage of two thousand years of Christian history, with its many peaks and valleys. Humankind's own tumultuous and violent history, especially that of the Christian church, should give us some pause for reflection and the beginning of wisdom. What is God's intent? The redemption of humanity and the cosmos. That should be our interpretive lens. There is nothing in apocalyptic theology that demands that our outlook be sectarian or exclusive.

Pablo Richard's conclusions concerning the nature and purpose of the Book of Revelation can be applied to apocalyptic writings in general, and it bears repeating:

> Revelation should be understood in the historical context in which it arose (Asia Minor at the close of the first century) and must be interpreted in the Spirit in which it was written (see Vatican II, *Dei Verbum,* no. 12). The book of Revelation is not abstract, universal, and eternal, equally valid for all ages and everywhere. Nor does it contain in enigmatic code form all of history from John to the end of the world. It is not a news report of the future nor is it science fiction. We reject every kind of fundamentalist, dispensationalist, or neoconservative interpretation of Revelation. We seek to interpret it in a positive manner in its literal and historical meaning, but we are likewise striving to interpret our present era in the light of Revelation. That is what we call the spiritual sense of Scripture.[1]

Notes

Introduction

1. D. S. Russell, *Apocalyptic: Ancient and Modern* (Philadelphia: Fortress Press, 1978), 1.

2. J. Christiaan Beker, *Paul's Apocalyptic Gospel: The Coming Triumph of God* (Philadelphia: Fortress Press, 1982), 24–25.

1. The Mother of All Theology

1. Klaus Koch, "What Is Apocalyptic? An Attempt at a Preliminary Definition," in *Visionaries and Their Apocalypses,* edited by Paul Hanson (Philadelphia: Fortress Press, 1983), 16–36. Reprint from the author's *The Rediscovery of Apocalyptic* (London, 1972). German scholars of the nineteenth century did a fair amount of research on the apocalyptic genre, although most of them continued to view it as essentially a negative phenomenon. Richard Sturm, "Defining the Word 'Apocalyptic': A Problem in Biblical Criticism," in *Apocalyptic and the New Testament. Essays in Honor of J. Louis Martyn,* edited by Joel Marcus and Marion Soards (Sheffield: JSOT Press, 1989), 17–48.

2. Albert Schweitzer, *The Quest of the Historical Jesus: A Critical Study of Its Progress from Reimarus to Wrede,* edited by James M. Robinson, translated by W. B. D. Montgomery, reprint, 1968 (Baltimore: Johns Hopkins University Press, 1998), 4. Note that Schweitzer uses the term *eschatology* to denote what would now describe by *apocalyptic.*

3. Schweitzer, *Quest,* 355–97.

4. Ibid., 370–71.

5. Ibid., 399, 402.

6. Ibid., 403.

7. Ernst Käsemann, "On the Subject of Primitive Christian Apocalyptic," in *New Testament Questions of Today* (Philadelphia: Fortress Press, 1969), 108–37.

8. Ernst Käsemann, "The Beginnings of Christian Theology," in *New Testament Questions of Today* (Philadelphia: Fortress Press, 1969), 82–107.

9. Käsemann, "Beginnings," 84.

10. Käsemann, "Primitive Christian Apocalyptic," 119–20.

11. Käsemann, "Beginnings," 100–101.

12. Ibid., 101–2.

13. Ibid., 105.

14. H. H. Rowley, *The Relevance of Apocalyptic* (London: Athlone, 1944), 13–16.

15. D. S. Russell, *The Method and Message of Jewish Apocalyptic* (Philadelphia: Westminster, 1964), 104–6.

16. D. S. Russell, *Divine Disclosure. An Introduction to Jewish Apocalyptic* (London, 1992), 8–13.

17. Koch, "What Is Apocalyptic?" 16–36.

18. Ibid., 21–24.

19. Ibid., 25–26.

20. Ibid., 27–28.

21. Ibid., 29.

22. Ibid.

23. Paul D. Hanson, *The Dawn of Apocalyptic: The Historical and Sociological Roots of Jewish Apocalyptic Eschatology* (Philadelphia: Fortress Press, 1983), 7, 11–12.

24. Paul Hanson, "Apocalypses and Apocalypticism," in *Anchor Bible Dictionary* (New York: Doubleday, 1992).

25. Hanson, *Dawn of Apocalyptic,* 430–33.

26. Hanson, "Apocalypses."

27. Richard Horsley, *Jesus and the Spiral of Violence: Popular Jewish Resistance in Roman Palestine* (Minneapolis: Fortress Press, 1987), 121–45.

28. Ibid., 143–44.

29. Christopher Rowland, *The Open Heaven: A Study of Apocalyptic in Judaism and Early Christianity* (London: SPCK, 1982), 11.

30. Ibid., 23–29.

31. Rowland, *Open Heaven,* 70–71. Rowland recognizes, of course, that an understanding of the present is the purpose of this genre: "…it is hardly surprising that at a later stage of her history the distinctive beliefs about God and history should have demanded an understanding of the Jewish nation's role in history, the relationship of the divine promises to the circumstances of the present, and the conviction that there was a divine dimension to human existence, however obscure it may seem in the present. Jewish apocalyptic sought to provide such an understanding of history and this theological conviction."

32. Philip Vielhauer, "Apocalyptic in Early Christianity," revised by George Strecker, in *New Testament Apocrypha,* edited by William Schneemelcher, translated by R. McL. Wilson (Louisville: Westminster/John Knox Press, 1992 [rev. ed.]), 549–54.

33. John J. Collins, ed., *Apocalypse: The Morphology of a Genre* (Missoula, Mont.: Scholars Press, 1979), 6–8.

34. John J. Collins, "Genre, Ideology and Social Movements in Jewish Apocalypticism," in *Mysteries and Revelations* (Sheffield: Sheffield University Press, 1991), 19. The article by A. Y. Collins appeared in *Semeia* 36, 1986, p. 7, and was reprinted in Adela Yarbro Collins, "Cosmology and Eschatology," in *Cosmology and Eschatology in Jewish and Christian Apocalypticism* (Leiden: Brill, 2000), 7.

35. John J. Collins, *The Apocalyptic Imagination: An Introduction to Jewish Apocalyptic Literature* (Grand Rapids, Mich.: Eerdmans, 1998), 4.

36. Paul B. Decock, "Some Issues in Apocalyptic in the Exegetical Literature of the Last Ten Years," *Neotestamentica* 33, no. 1 (1999): 26–27.

37. D. S. Sim, *Apocalyptic Eschatology in the Gospel of Matthew* (Cambridge: Cambridge University Press, 1996).

38. George W. E. Nickelsburg, "The Apocalyptic Construction of Reality in 1 Enoch," in *Mysteries and Revelations: Apocalyptic Studies Since the Uppsala Colloquium,* eds. John J. and Fishbane Collins, M. (Sheffield: Sheffield University Press, 1991), 51–64.

39. Martha Himmelfarb, "Revelation and Rapture: The Transformation of the Visionary in the Ascent Apocalypses," in *Mysteries and Revelations: Apocalyptic Studies Since the Uppsala Colloquium,* eds. John J. and Fishbane Collins, M. (Sheffield: Sheffield University Press, 1991), 89–90.

40. John J. Collins, "Genre, Ideology and Social Movements," 15–17.

41. M. Eugene Boring, *Revelation: Interpretation* (Louisville: John Knox Press, 1989), 52–54.

2. Jesus and the End of the Ages

1. Kloppenborg does not claim that Q or Q_1 should enjoy any privileged status, but that its integrity as an independent interpretation of the tradition be respected when engaging in reconstructions of the historical Jesus. He also denies that reconstructions of Q and its development can or should be translated naively into statements about the historical Jesus.

2. John S. Kloppenborg Verbin, *Excavating Q: The History and Settings of the Sayings Gospel* (Edinburgh: T & T Clark, 2000), 2. "If Q is a viable literary hypothesis and if modern reconstructions of Q approximate its original shape, the understandings of gospel origins and the nature of the early Jesus movement need to be refined to accommodate this additional complexity. We must take account of an early expression of the Jesus tradition that did not feel the urgency of accounting for his death in soteriological terms. We must take account of a document that drew heavily upon Deuteronomistic theology, visible only incidentally in Mark or 1 Thessalonians. We must take account of a document that privileged sayings rather than wondrous deeds and, in accord with this emphasis, the heavenly Sophia. We must take account of a sector of the Jesus movement rather unlike the urban Pauline churches, characterized by a distinctive—even radical—social practice. And we must take notice of a document that grounded its practice not in a once-and-for-all "Christ event" but in relation to the epic history of Israel."

3. Kloppenborg Verbin, *Excavating Q,* 3. Kloppenborg does not quarrel with the fact that Q is a hypothesis: "Precisely because Q is professedly the product of a hypothesis, scholarship on Q nicely exemplifies the intellectual process of trying to make sense of the diversity and particularity of historical data." Several scholars, among them Mark Goodacre, Michael Goulder, Edward Hobbs, H. B. Green, and E. P. Sanders espouse what is called the Farrer Hypothesis. This hypothesis accepts the priority of Mark, but rejects the existence of Q in the

development of Matthew and Luke. Visit the web site devoted to this hypothesis, "Mark without Q," at: http://www.ntgateway.com/q for an extensive discussion and bibliography.

4. Adela Yarbro Collins, "Cosmology and Eschatology," in *Cosmology and Eschatology in Jewish and Christian Apocalypticism* (Leiden: Brill, 2000), 145. For a thorough discussion of the recent studies on the Son of Man in the Gospels, see John R. Donahue, "Recent Studies on the Origin of 'Son of Man' in the Gospels," *Catholic Biblical Quarterly* 48 (1986): 484–98.

5. Adela Yarbro Collins, "The Influence of Daniel on the New Testament," in *Daniel: A Commentary on the Book of Daniel,* John J. Collins (Minneapolis: Fortress Press, 1993), 90–105.

6. John J. Collins, *The Apocalyptic Imagination: An Introduction to Jewish Apocalyptic Literature* (Grand Rapids, Mich.: Eerdmans, 1998), 261–63.

7. A. Y. Collins, "Cosmology and Eschatology," 154–56, 195.

8. John J. Collins, *The Apocalyptic Imagination.,* 263.

9. E. P. Sanders, *Jesus and Judaism* (Philadelphia: Fortress Press, 1985), 327.

10. Ibid., 97.

11. E. P. Sanders, "The Genre of Palestinian Jewish Apocalypses," in *Apocalypticism in the Mediterranean World and the Near East,* Proceedings of the International Colloquium on Apocalypticism Uppsala, August 12–17, 1979, edited by David Hellholm (Tübingen: J. C. B. Mohr [Paul Siebeck], 1983), 456.

12. Sanders, *Jesus and Judaism,* 319.

13. Ibid., 324.

14. Ibid., 118, 323–26.

15. Ibid., 72–73, 75.

16. Paula Fredriksen, *Jesus of Nazareth. King of the Jews* (New York: Vintage Books, 1999), 270.

17. Ibid., 225–32.

18. Ibid., 94–95. Fredriksen follows Sanders' line of reasoning regarding the Twelve; namely, that it is a symbol of the totality of Israel. Matthew 19:28 illustrates that the Twelve would play a role in the Kingdom, especially in judging Israel.

19. Ibid., 132.

20. Ibid., 262–64. "The disciples' conviction that they had seen the Risen Christ, their permanent relocation to Jerusalem, their principled inclusion of Gentiles *as* Gentiles—all these are historical bedrock, facts known past doubting about the earliest community after Jesus' death. They fall into a pattern. Each marks a point along the arc of apocalyptic hope that passes from Daniel to Paul, from Qumran's Scrolls to the synagogue's Eighteen Benedictions, from the prophets of the Jewish canon to the Book of Revelation, which concludes the New Testament: the conviction that God is good; that he is in control of history; that he will not countenance evil indefinitely. All the many and various themes in all these different writings unite around this fundamental belief that, at the End, God will prevail over evil, restoring and redeeming his creation."

21. N. T. Wright, *Jesus and the Victory of God* (Minneapolis: Fortress, 1996), 96.

22. Ibid., 207.

23. Ibid., 512–13.

24. Dale C. Allison, "Jesus & the Victory of Apocalyptic," in *Jesus and the Restoration of Israel: A Critical Assessment of N. T. Wright's "Jesus and the Victory of God,"* edited by Carey C. Newman (Downers Grove, Ill.: InterVarsity Press, 1999), 126–41.

25. Marcus J. Borg, "A Temperate Case for a Non-Eschatological Jesus," in *Jesus in Contemporary Scholarship* (Valley Forge, Pa.: Trinity Press International, 1994), 47–68.

26. Ibid., 51–53.

27. Richard Horsley, *Jesus and the Spiral of Violence: Popular Jewish Resistance in Roman Palestine* (Minneapolis: Fortress Press, 1987), 490–91.

28. Borg, "Non-Eschatological Jesus," 53–58.

29. Marcus J. Borg, "Jesus and Eschatology: Current Reflections," in *Jesus in Contemporary Scholarship* (Valley Forge, Pa.: Trinity Press International, 1994), 69–96.

30. Ibid., 88–89.

31. John Dominic Crossan, *The Historical Jesus. The Life of a Mediterranean Jewish Peasant* (San Francisco: HarperSanFrancisco, 1991), xxvii–xxxiv. For a detailed description of the sources in the various strata, see pages 427–34.

32. Dale C. Allison, *Jesus of Nazareth: Millenarian Prophet* (Minneapolis: Fortress Press, 1998), 10–33; Wright, *Victory,* 47–61.

33. Crossan, *Historical Jesus,* 238. He goes on to state: "The advantage of using the wider, generic term and the narrower, more specific term is that it helps to understand their ready slippage from one to another. In discussing, therefore, those texts about the coming Son of Man, I am speaking about the apocalyptic Jesus and asking whether Jesus saw this figure against the darkening scenario of an imminent end to the world. And by end of the world I mean that the apocalypticist expected a divine intervention so transcendentally obvious that one's adversaries or enemies, oppressors or persecutors would be forced to acknowledge it and to accept conversion or concede defeat."

34. John Dominic Crossan, *Jesus: A Revolutionary Biography* (San Francisco: HarperSanFrancisco, 1994), 52.

35. Crossan, *Historical Jesus,* 234–37; Crossan, *Revolutionary,* 44–48.

36. Crossan, *Revolutionary,* 50; Crossan, *Historical Jesus,* 255. "Only six apocalyptic Son of Man texts have more than single attestation. Only with those six is it possible to establish a comparative trajectory and to see thereby the tradition's development. And the conclusion is very surprising. One could easily imagine an apocalyptic judgment in which Jesus was imagined as chief witness for the prosecution or even as the prosecuting attorney. But throughout this tradition Jesus is seen as the apocalyptic judge, and that may well have needed a very early use of Daniel 7:13 so that, just as its one who was ancient of days gave power and dominion to the one who was like a son of man, so now God cedes apocalyptic judgment to Jesus. *But what is extraordinary is that I could not find a single case within those six complexes in which two independent sources both contained the Son of Man designation for Jesus.*

37. Crossan, *Historical Jesus,* 255.

38. Ibid., 259.

39. Ibid., 421–22.

40. Bart D. Ehrman, *Jesus: Apocalyptic Prophet of the New Millennium* (Minneapolis: Fortress Press, 1999), 42–43.

41. Ibid., 114–23.

42. Ibid., 134–37.

43. Ibid., 139.

44. Ibid., 141–62.

45. Dale C. Allison, "The Eschatology of Jesus," in *The Encyclopedia of Apocalypticism,* edited by John J. Collins (New York: Continuum, 1998), 267–302.

46. Ibid., 293–98.

47. Ibid., 275.

48. Allison, *Jesus of Nazareth,* 172–73.

49. Ibid., 189–96.

50. Ibid., 201–7.

3. Paul's "Apocalyptic Gospel"

1. Albert Schweitzer, *The Mysticism of Paul the Apostle,* translated by B. D. Montgomery, William, with a preface by Jaroslav Pelikan, reprint, 1931 (Baltimore: Johns Hopkins University Press, 1998), 80–82.

2. Ibid., 90.

3. Ibid., 92–93.

4. Ibid., 99.

5. Ibid., 384.

6. Martinus C. de Boer, "Paul and Apocalyptic Eschatology," in *The Encyclopedia of Apocalyptic,* edited by John J. Collins (New York: Continuum, 1998), 361–63. De Boer refers to Bultmann's "New Testament and Mythology," in *New Testament and Mythology and Other Basic Writings,* edited by S. Ogden, 1–43 (Philadelphia: Fortress Press, 1984).

7. Ernst Käsemann, "On the Subject of Primitive Christian Apocalyptic," in *New Testament Questions of Today* (Philadelphia, 1969), 135–36.

8. J. Christiaan Beker, *Paul's Apocalyptic Gospel: The Coming Triumph of God.* (Philadelphia: Fortress Press, 1982), 19.

9. Ibid., 30–53.

10. J. Christiaan Beker, *The Triumph of God: The Essence of Paul's Thought,* translated by Loren T. Stuckenbruck (Minneapolis: Fortress, 1990), 40–41.

11. J. Christiaan Beker, *Paul the Apostle: The Triumph of God in Life and Thought* (Edinburgh: T & T Clark, 1980), 135.

12. Ibid., 145.

13. Ibid., 61–62.

14. Beker, *Paul the Apostle,* xiii–xiv; Beker, *The Triumph of God,* 15–19.

15. Beker, *The Triumph of God,* 72–73.

16. Beker, *Paul the Apostle,* 148.

17. Beker, *The Triumph of God,* 80–86.

18. Vincent Branick, "Apocalyptic Paul?" *Catholic Biblical Quarterly* 47 (1985): 664–75.

19. Ibid., 672–73.

20. Ibid., 674.

21. Leander E. Keck, "Paul and Apocalyptic Theology," *Interpretation* 38 (1984): 229–41.

22. Ibid., 237.

23. Keck, "Paul and Apocalyptic Theology," 238. Paul envisions these powers as being subjected rather than annihilated, as in 1 Corinthians 15:24.

24. Keck, "Paul and Apocalyptic Theology," 240–41.

25. J. Louis Martyn, *Theological Issues in the Letters of Paul* (Nashville: Abingdon Press, 1997), 87.

26. J. Louis Martyn, "Apocalyptic Antinomies in Paul's Letter to the Galatians," in *Theological Issues in the Letter of Paul* (Nashville: Abingdon Press, 1997), 111–24.

27. J. Louis Martyn, "God's Way of Making Right What Is Wrong," in *Theological Issues in the Letters of Paul* (Nashville: Abingdon Press, 1997), 151.

28. J. Louis Martyn, "Epistemology at the Turn of the Ages," in *Theological Issues in the Letters of Paul* (Nashville: Abingdon Press, 1997), 92–94. This juncture is seen in 2 Corinthians 2:14–17; 3:1–18; 4:1—5:10; 4:1–15; 4:16—5:5; 5:6–1; 5:11–15; 5:16–21; and 6:1–10.

29. de Boer, "Paul and Apocalyptic." Schweitzer concentrated on 1 Enoch; Psalms of Solomon; 2 Baruch; 4 Ezra; Jubilees; Testament of the Twelve Patriarchs; and the Assumption of Moses.

30. de Boer, "Paul and Apocalyptic," 350.

31. Ibid., 351.

32. de Boer, "Paul and Apocalyptic," 357. Paul uses *apokalypsis* to refer to several things: the divine mysteries; the parousia; and the power of God for salvation.

33. de Boer, "Paul and Apocalyptic," 358. This is also reflected in his 1989 work "Paul and Jewish Apocalyptic Eschatology," in *Apocalyptic and the New Testament: Essays in Honor of J. Louis Martyn,* edited by Joel Marcus and Marion Soards. JSNTSS 24 (Sheffield: JSOT Press, 1989), 169–90.

34. de Boer, "Paul and Apocalyptic," 359–60. Examples of this type of cosmological pattern are found in Genesis 6:1–6; 1 Enoch 6—19; 64:1–2; 69:4–5; 86:1–6; 106:13–17; Jubilees 4:15, 22; 5:1–8; 10:4–5; Testament of Reuben 5:6–7; Testament of Naphtali 3:5; CD 2:17—3:1; 2 Baruch 56:12–15; Lib Ant Bib 34:1–5; Wisdom 2:23–24; Jude 6; 2 Peter 2:4.

35. de Boer, "Paul and Apocalyptic," 359–60. This is found in 4 Ezra and 2 Baruch, both of which emphasize the fall and responsibility of Adam: 4 Ezra 3:5–7, 20–21; 4:30–31; 7:118–19; 2 Baruch 17:2–3; 23:4; 48:42–43; 54:14, 19; 56:6; cf. 1 Enoch 69:6; Jubilees 3:17–25; 4:29–30; *LAB* 13:8–9; Sirach 25:24; Wisdom 10:1.

36. See 1QS 1—4; 1QM; CD.

37. de Boer, "Paul and Apocalyptic," 360–61. He refers to the "god of this age" in 2 Corinthians 4:4 and "Beliar" in 2 Corinthians 6:15. The references to "the rulers of this age" in 1 Corinthians 2:6–8; the "principalities and powers" in Romans 8:38 and 1 Corinthians 15:24; and Paul's personification of Sin and Death as oppressive powers that enslave humans in Romans 5:12, 21 and 1 Corinthians 15:26, 56 are probably further expressions of this cosmological eschatology.

38. Martinus C. de Boer, *The Defeat of Death: Apocalyptic Eschatology in 1 Corinthians 15 and Romans 5,* Journal for the Study of the New Testament Supplement Series 22 (Sheffield: JSOT Press, 1988), 83–91, 181–82.

39. Ibid., 183.

40. de Boer, "Paul and Apocalyptic," 370.

41. Paul Segal, *Paul the Convert: The Apostolate and Apostasy of Saul the Pharisee* (New Haven: Yale University Press, 1990), 34–71; C. R. Morray-Jones, "Paradise Revisited (2 Cor 12:1–12): The Jewish Mystical Background of Paul's Apostolate, Part I: The Jewish Sources," *Harvard Theological Review* 86, no. 2 (1993): 177–217; C. R. Morray-Jones, "Part 2: Paul's Heavenly Ascent and Its Significance," *Harvard Theological Review* 86, no. 3 (1993): 265–92; James D. Tabor, *Things Unutterable: Paul's Ascent to Paradise in Its Greco-Roman, Judaic, and*

Early Christian Contexts (Lanham, Md.: University Press of America, 1986), 32–34.

42. Joseph Plevnik, *Paul and the Parousia: An Exegetical and Theological Investigation* (Peabody, Mass.: Hendrickson, 1997).

43. Ibid., 323–27.

44. Alexandra Brown, *The Cross and Human Transformation: Paul's Apocalyptic Word in 1 Corinthians* (Minneapolis: Fortress Press, 1995), 97–105.

45. Ibid., 145–46.

46. Ibid., 147.

47. Ibid., 164–65.

4. Apocalypse Now

1. Duane F. Watson, "Millennium," in *Eerdmans Dictionary of the Bible,* edited by David Noel Freedman (Grand Rapids, Mich.: Eerdmans, 2000), 900–901. See Paul Duff, "Reading the Apocalypse at the Millennium," *Religious Studies Review* 26, no. 3 (July 2000), 217–22. Duff provides a good representative survey of some modern commentaries on the Book of Revelation.

2. M. Eugene Boring, *Revelation: Interpretation* (Louisville: John Knox Press, 1989), 47–50.

3. Edward F. Edinger, *Archetype of the Apocalypse: A Jungian Study on the Book of Revelation* (Chicago: Open Court, 1999), xiii–xx.

4. Bart D. Ehrman, *Jesus: Apocalyptic Prophet of the New Millennium* (Minneapolis: Fortress Press, 1999), 14–15.

5. Ibid., 7–10.

6. Adela Yarbro Collins, "The Influence of Daniel on the New Testament," in *Daniel: A Commentary on the Book of Daniel,* John J. Collins, Hermeneia (Minneapolis: Fortress Press, 1993), 105; John E. Goldingay, *Daniel,* Word Biblical Commentary (Dallas: Word Publishing, 1987), xxix.

7. Goldingay, *Daniel,* xxix–xxxviii.

8. Ibid., 320–22.

9. Goldingay, *Daniel,* 326–27; Louis Hartman and Alexander DiLella, *The Book of Daniel,* Anchor Bible (Garden City, N.Y.: Doubleday, 1978), 53; John J. Collins, *The Apocalyptic Imagination: An*

Introduction to Jeswish Apocalyptic Literature (Grand Rapids, Mich.: Eerdmans, 1998), 85–90.

10. Collins, *The Apocalyptic Imagination*, 114–15; John J. Collins, *Daniel: A Commentary on the Book of Daniel*, Hermeneia (Minneapolis: Fortress Press, 1993), 59–61; Hartman, *Daniel*, 52–53; Goldingay, *Daniel*, 320–21. Collins describes the work as a "highly imaginative reconstruction" of the historical crisis, partially shaped by mythic paradigms.

11. Leonard Thompson, *The Book of Revelation: Apocalypse and Empire* (New York: Oxford University Press, 1990), 95–107.

12. Leonard Thompson, *Revelation* (Nashville: Abingdon Press, 1998), 30–34.

13. Thompson, *Apocalypse and Empire*, 74–91.

14. Adela Yarbro Collins, *Crisis and Catharsis: The Power of the Apocalypse* (Philadelphia: Westminster Press, 1984), 49–50.

15. Ibid., 76–77.

16. Ibid., 104–7.

17. Ibid., 111–38.

18. Ibid., 160–61. This is perhaps best expressed by the following: "The task of Revelation was to overcome the unbearable tension perceived by the author between what was and what ought to have been. His purpose was to create that tension for readers unaware of it, to heighten it for those who felt it already, and then to overcome it in an act of literary imagination. In the literary creation which is the Apocalypse, the tension between what was and what ought to be is manifest in the opposition between symbols of God's rule and symbols of Satan's rule, between symbols of the authority and power of Christ and symbols of the authority and power of Caesar"(page 141).

19. Ibid., 165–75.

20. Elisabeth Schüssler-Fiorenza, *The Book of Revelation: Justice and Judgment* (Philadelphia: Fortress Press, 1985), 3. "The generative center of Rev. is not the course of history but the experience of the Christian community in the christologically qualified end time. In ever new visions and images the author 'interprets' prophetically the concrete situation of Christians in Asia Minor at the short time before the end."

21. Ibid., 8.

22. Ibid., 7–8.

23. Ibid., 183.

24. Ibid., 187–89.

25. Ibid., 198.

26. David Aune, *Revelation,* Word Biblical Commentary (Dallas, Tex.: Word Books, 1997), lxix.

27. Ibid., cxviii–cxxxiv.

28. G. K. Beale, *The Book of Revelation,* The New International Greek Testament Commentary (Grand Rapids, Mich.: Eerdmans, 1999), 48–49.

29. Ibid., 56.

30. Ibid., 69.

31. Ibid., 38–39.

32. Ibid., 33.

33. Ibid., 173–74.

34. Catherine Gonzalez and Justo Gonzalez, *Revelation* (Louisville, Ky.: Westminster John Knox Press, 1997), 1–11.

35. Richard Bauckham, *The Theology of the Book of Revelation* (Cambridge: Cambridge University Press, 1993), 18.

36. Ibid., 7. "The effect of John's visions, one might say, is to expand his readers' world, both spatially (into heaven) and temporally (into the eschatological future), or, to put it another way, to open their world to divine transcendence."

37. Ibid., 20–21.

38. Ibid., 15.

39. Bruce J. Malina and John J. Pilch, *Social-Science Commentary on the Book of Revelation* (Minneapolis: Fortress Press, 2000), 4.

40. Ibid., 10–11.

41. Ibid., 10–12.

42. Wes Howard-Brook and Anthony Gwyther, *Unveiling Empire: Reading Revelation Then and Now* (Maryknoll, N.Y.: Orbis Books, 1999), 116–17.

43. Ibid., 157–58.

44. Ibid., 183–85.

45. Brian K. Blount, "Reading Revelation Today: Witness as Active Resistance," *Interpretation* 54, no. 4 (2000): 398–412.

46. David Barr, *Tales of the End: A Narrative Commentary on the Book of Revelation* (Santa Rosa, Calif.: Polebridge Press, 1998), 1–4.

47. Ibid., 13–15.

48. Ibid., 148–49.

49. Ibid., 179–80.

50. Ibid., 23–24.

5. Apocalyptic, the World, and the Church

1. David Jacobsen, *Preaching in the New Creation: The Promise of New Testament Apocalyptic Texts* (Louisville, Ky.: Westminster John Knox Press, 1999).

2. Ibid., 43–44, 102.

3. J. Christiaan Beker, *Paul's Apocalyptic Gospel: The Coming Triumph of God* (Philadelphia: Fortress Press, 1982), 110.

4. Ibid., 119.

5 Ibid., 120.

6. Ibid., 105.

7. Ibid., 105–10.

8. Elisabeth Schüssler-Fiorenza, "The Phenomenon of Early Christian Apocalyptic: Some Reflections on Method," in *Apocalypticism in the Mediterranean World and the Near East,* Proceedings of the International Colloquium on Apocalypticism Uppsala, August 12–17, 1979, edited by David Hellholm (Tübingen: J. C. B. Mohr [Paul Siebeck], 1983), 295–316.

9. Ibid., 309–12.

10. Walter Wink, *The Powers That Be: Theology for a New Millennium* (New York: Doubleday, 1998).

11. Ibid., 81.

12. Ibid., 112–45.

13. Allan A. Boesak, *Comfort and Protest: The Apocalypse from a South African Perspective* (Philadelphia: Westminster Press, 1987).

14. Ibid., 18.

15. Ibid., 28–29.

16. Pablo Richard, *Apocalypse: A People's Commentary on the Book of Revelation* (Maryknoll, N.Y.: Orbis Press, 1995), 3.

17. Ibid., 3–5.

18. Beker, *Paul's Apocalyptic Gospel,* 35.

19. M. Eugene Boring, "The Language of Universal Salvation in Paul," *Journal of Biblical Literature* 105 (1986): 209. 1 Corinthians 1:18 is a fine example of the first type: "For the word of the cross is folly

to those who are perishing, but to us who are being saved it is the power of God"; on the other hand, Romans 5:18 proclaims: "Then as one man's trespass led to condemnation for all men, so one man's act of righteousness leads to acquittal and life for all men." Other texts: for limited salvation, 1 Thessalonians 1:10; 4:13–17; 5:3–9; 1 Corinthians 1:21–31; 3:16–17; 9:22; 11:32; 15:18; 2 Corinthians 2:15–16; 4:3; 5:10; Galatians 3:10, 23–29; 5:19–21; Romans 1:16–17; 2:1–16; 2:21–25; 8:5–8; 9:2; 10:1. Universal salvation is implied in 1 Corinthians 15:22–28; 2 Corinthians 5:19; Romans 5:12–21; 11:26–36; Philippians 2:6–11.

20. Boring, "Universal Salvation," 269–92. Boring also shows that one of the reasons that Pauline scholars differ on this issue is that often they subordinate either the particularistic passages to the universalist ones, or vice versa, according to their individual views. Paul will not admit of such neat definitions.

21. J. Christiaan Beker, *Paul the Apostle:* The Triumph of God in Life and Thought (Edinburgh: T & T Clark, 1980), 193–94; Boring, "Universal Salvation," 270–73.

22. E. P. Sanders, *Paul and Palestinian Judaism: A Comparison of Patterns of Religion* (Philadelphia: Fortress Press, 1977), 434–35; 438–40; 453–63; 520–23; 549–52; 515–19; in Boring, "Universal Salvation," 274.

23. Boring, "Universal Salvation," 274–75.

24. Ibid., 288.

25. Ibid., 290–92.

26. Martinus C. de Boer, "Paul and Apocalyptic Eschatology," in *The Encyclopedia of Apocalyptic,* edited by John J. Collins (New York: Continuum, 1998), 371–74.

6. Conclusion

1. Pablo Richard, *Apocalypse: A People's Commentary on the Book of Revelation (Maryknoll, N.Y.: Orbis Press, 1995),* 5.

Bibliography

Allison, Dale C. "The Eschatology of Jesus." In *The Encyclopedia of Apocalypticism,* edited by John J. Collins, 267–302. New York: Continuum, 1998.

———. *Jesus of Nazareth: Millenarian Prophet.* Minneapolis: Fortress Press, 1998.

———. "Jesus & the Victory of Apocalyptic." In *Jesus and the Restoration of Israel:. A Critical Assessment of N. T. Wright's "Jesus and the Victory of God,"* edited by Carey C. Newman, 126–41. Downers Grove, Ill.: InterVarsity Press, 1999.

Aune, David. *Revelation.* Word Biblical Commentary. Dallas, Tex.: Word Books, 1997.

———. *Revelation 17–22.* Word Biblical Commentary. Dallas, Tex.: Word Books, 1998.

———. *Revelation 6–16.* Word Biblical Commentary. Dallas, Tex.: Word Books, 1998.

Barr, David. *Tales of the End: A Narrative Commentary on the Book of Revelation.* Santa Rosa, Calif.: Polebridge Press, 1998.

Bauckham, Richard. *The Climax of Prophecy.* Edinburgh: T & T Clark, 1993.

———. *The Theology of the Book of Revelation.* Cambridge: Cambridge University Press, 1993.

Beale, G. K. *The Book of Revelation.* The New International Greek Testament Commentary. Grand Rapids, Mich.: Eerdmans, 1999.

Beker, J. Christiaan. *Paul the Apostle: The Triumph of God in Life and Thought.* Edinburgh: T & T Clark, 1980.

―――. *Paul's Apocalyptic Gospel: The Coming Triumph of God.* Philadelphia: Fortress Press, 1982.

―――. *The Triumph of God: The Essence of Paul's Thought.* Translated by Loren T. Stuckenbruck. Minneapolis: Fortress Press, 1990.

Blount, Brian K. "Reading Revelation Today: Witness as Active Resistance." *Interpretation* 54, no. 4 (2000): 398–412.

Boesak, Allan A. *Comfort and Protest: The Apocalypse from a South African Perspective.* Philadelphia: Westminster Press, 1987.

Borg, Marcus J. "Jesus and Eschatology: Current Reflections." In *Jesus in Contemporary Scholarship,* 69–96. Valley Forge, Pa.: Trinity Press International, 1994.

―――. "A Temperate Case for a Non-Eschatological Jesus." In *Jesus in Contemporary Scholarship,* 47–68. Valley Forge, Pa.: Trinity Press International, 1994.

Boring, M. Eugene. "The Language of Universal Salvation in Paul." *Journal of Biblical Literature* 105 (1986): 269–92.

―――. *Revelation.* Interpretation. Louisville: John Knox Press, 1989.

Branick, Vincent. "Apocalyptic Paul?" *Catholic Biblical Quarterly* 47 (1985): 664–75.

Brown, Alexandra. *The Cross and Human Transformation: Paul's Apocalyptic Word in 1 Corinthians.* Minneapolis: Fortress Press, 1995.

Charlesworth, James H., ed. *The Old Testament Pseudepigrapha.* Vol. 1, Apocalyptic Literature and Testaments. Garden City, New York: Doubleday, 1983.

————, ed. *The Old Testament Pseudepigrapha.* 2 vols. Garden City, New York: Doubleday, 1985.

Collins, Adela Yarbro. *Crisis and Catharsis: The Power of the Apocalypse.* Philadelphia: Westminster Press, 1984.

————. "Apocalypses and Apocalypticism: Early Christian." In *Anchor Bible Dictionary,* 1:288–91. Doubleday, 1992.

————. "The Influence of Daniel on the New Testament." In *Daniel: A Commentary on the Book of Daniel,* John J. Collins, 90–123. Minneapolis: Fortress Press, 1993.

————. *Cosmology and Eschatology in Jewish and Christian Apocalypticism.* Leiden: Brill, 2000.

Collins, John J., ed. *Apocalypse: The Morphology of a Genre.* Semeia. Missoula, Mont.: Scholars Press, 1979.

————, ed. *The Encyclopedia of Apocalypticism.* Vol. 1. New York: Continuum, 1998.

————. "Genre, Ideology and Social Movements in Jewish Apocalypticism." In *Mysteries and Revelations,* 11–32. Sheffield: Sheffield University Press, 1991.

————. *Daniel: A Commentary on the Book of Daniel.* Hermeneia. Minneapolis: Fortress Press, 1993.

————. *The Apocalyptic Imagination: An Introduction to Jewish Apocalyptic Literature.* Grand Rapids, Mich.: Eerdmans, 1998, rev. ed.

Collins, John J. and James H. Charlesworth, eds. *Mysteries and Revelations: Apocalyptic Studies Since the Uppsala Colloquium.* Journal for the Study of the Pseudepigrapha Supplement Series 9. Sheffield: University of Sheffield Press, 1991.

Crossan, John Dominic. *The Historical Jesus: The Life of a Mediterranean Jewish Peasant.* San Francisco: HarperSanFrancisco, 1991.

————. *Jesus: A Revolutionary Biography.* San Francisco: HarperSan-Francisco, 1994.

de Boer, Martinus C. *The Defeat of Death: Apocalyptic Eschatology in 1 Corinthians 15 and Romans 5.* Journal for the Study of the New Testament Supplement Series 22. Sheffield: JSOT Press, 1988.

————. "Paul and Jewish Apocalyptic Eschatology." In *Apocalyptic and the New Testament: Essays in Honor of J. Louis Martyn,* eds. Joel Marcus and Marion L. Soards. Journal for the Study of the New Testament Supplement Series 24, 169–90. Sheffield: Sheffield Academic Press, 1989.

————. "Paul and Apocalyptic Eschatology." In *The Encyclopedia of Apocalyptic,* edited by John J. Collins, 345–83. New York: Continuum, 1998.

Decock, Paul B. "Some Issues in Apocalyptic in the Exegetical Literature of the Last Ten Years." *Neotestamentica* 33, no. 1 (1999): 1–31.

Donahue, John R. "Recent Studies on the Origin of 'Son of Man' in the Gospels." *Catholic Biblical Quarterly* 48 (1986): 484–98.

Duff, Paul. "Reading the Apocalypse at the Millennium." *Religious Studies Review* 26, no. 3 (July 2000): 217–22.

Duling, Dennis C. "Millennialism." In *The Social Sciences and New Testament Interpretation,* edited by Richard Rohrbaugh, 183–205. Peabody, Mass.: Hendrickson, 1996.

Edinger, Edward F. *Archetype of the Apocalypse: A Jungian Study on the Book of Revelation.* Chicago: Open Court, 1999.

Ehrman, Bart D. *Jesus: Apocalyptic Prophet of the New Millennium.* Minneapolis: Fortress Press, 1999.

Fredriksen, Paula. *Jesus of Nazareth: King of the Jews.* New York: Vintage Books, 1999.

Goldingay, John E. *Daniel.* Word Biblical Commentary. Dallas: Word Publishing, 1987.

Gonzalez, Catherine, and Justo Gonzalez. *Revelation.* Louisville, Ky.: Westminster John Knox Press, 1997.

Hanson, Paul. "Apocalypses and Apocalypticism." In *Anchor Bible Dictionary,* 1:279–82. New York: Doubleday, 1992.

Hanson, Paul D. *The Dawn of Apocalyptic: The Historical and Sociological Roots of Jewish Apocalyptic Eschatology.* Philadelphia: Fortress Press, 1983.

Hartman, Louis, and Alexander DiLella. *The Book of Daniel.* Anchor Bible. Garden City, N. Y.: Doubleday, 1978.

Hellholm, D., ed. *Apocalypticism in the Mediterranean World and the Near East:* Proceedings of the International Colloquium on Apocalypticism, Uppsala, August 12–17, 1979. Tübingen: Mohr (Siebeck), 1983.

Himmelfarb, Martha. "Revelation and Rapture: The Transformation of the Visionary in the Ascent Apocalypses." In *Mysteries and Revelations: Apocalyptic Studies Since the Uppsala Colloquium,* eds. John J. and Fishbane M. Collins, 79–90. Sheffield: Sheffield University Press, 1991.

Horsley, Richard. *Jesus and the Spiral of Violence: Popular Jewish Resistance in Roman Palestine.* Minneapolis: Fortress Press, 1987.

Howard-Brook, Wes, and Anthony Gwyther. *Unveiling Empire: Reading Revelation Then and Now.* Maryknoll, N. Y.: Orbis Books, 1999.

Jacobsen, David Schnasa. *Preaching in the New Creation.* Louisville, Ky.: Westminster John Knox Press, 1999.

Käsemann, Ernst. "The Beginnings of Christian Theology." In *New Testament Questions of Today,* 82–107. Philadelphia: Fortress Press, 1969.

————. "On the Subject of Primitive Christian Apocalyptic." In *New Testament Questions of Today,* 108–37. Philadelphia: Fortress Press, 1969.

Keck, Leander E. "Paul and Apocalyptic Theology." *Interpretation* 38 (1984): 229–41.

Kloppenborg, John. "Symbolic Eschatology and the Apocalypticism of Q." *Harvard Theological Review* 80, no. 3 (1987): 287–306.

————. "The Sayings Gospel Q and the Quest of the Historical Jesus." *Harvard Theological Review* 89, no. 4 (1996): 307–44.

Kloppenborg Verbin, John S. *Excavating Q: The History and Settings of the Sayings Gospel.* Edinburgh: T & T Clark, 2000.

Koch, Klaus. "What Is Apocalyptic? An Attempt at a Preliminary Definition." In *Visionaries and Their Apocalypses,* edited by Paul Hanson, 16–36. Philadelphia: Fortress Press, 1983.

Malina, Bruce J., and John J. Pilch. *Social-Science Commentary on the Book of Revelation.* Minneapolis: Fortress Press, 2000.

Martyn, J. Louis. "Apocalyptic Antinomies in Paul's Letter to the Galatians." In *Theological Issues in the Letters of Paul,* 111–24. Nashville: Abingdon Press, 1997.

————. "Epistemology at the Turn of the Ages." In *Theological Issues in the Letters of Paul,* 89–110. Nashville: Abingdon Press, 1997.

————. "God's Way of Making Right What Is Wrong." In *Theological Issues in the Letters of Paul,* 141–56. Nashville: Abingdon Press, 1997.

————. *Theological Issues in the Letters of Paul.* Nashville: Abingdon Press, 1997.

McGinn, Bernard, ed. *The Encyclopedia of Apocalypticism.* Vol. 2. New York: Continuum, 1998.

Morray-Jones, C. R. "Paradise Revisited (2 Cor 12:1–12): The Jewish Mystical Background of Paul's Apostolate. Part 1: The Jewish

Sources." *Harvard Theological Review* 86, no. 2 (1993): 177–217.

————. "Part 2: Paul's Heavenly Ascent and Its Significance." *Harvard Theological Review* 86, no. 3 (1993): 265–92.

Newman, Carey C. *Jesus and the Restoration of Israel: A Critical Assessment of N. T. Wright's "Jesus and the Victory of God."* Downers Grove, Ill.: InterVarsity Press, 1999.

Nickelsburg, George W. E. "The Apocalyptic Construction of Reality in 1 Enoch." In *Mysteries and Revelations: Apocalyptic Studies Since the Uppsala Colloquium,* eds John J. and Fishbane M. Collins, 51–64. Sheffield: Sheffield University Press, 1991.

Perrin, Norman. *The New Testament—An Introduction: Proclamation and Parenesis, Myth and History.* New York: Harcourt Brace Jovanovich, 1974.

————. *Rediscovering the Teaching of Jesus.* New York: Harper & Row, 1976.

Plevnik, Joseph. *Paul and the Parousia: An Exegetical and Theological Investigation.* Peabody, Mass.: Hendrickson, 1997.

Reddish, Mitchell G. *Apocalyptic Literature: A Reader.* Peabody, Mass.: Hendrickson, 1995.

Richard, Pablo. *Apocalypse: A People's Commentary on the Book of Revelation.* Maryknoll, N.Y.: Orbis Press, 1995.

Rowland, Christopher. *The Open Heaven: A Study of Apocalyptic in Judaism and Early Christianity.* London: SPCK, 1982.

Rowley, H. H. *The Relevance of Apocalyptic.* London: Athlone, 1944.

Russell, D. S. *Apocalyptic: Ancient and Modern.* Philadelphia: Fortress Press, 1978.

————. *Divine Disclosure: An Introduction to Jewish Apocalyptic.* London: SCM Press, 1992.

Sanders, E. P. "The Genre of Palestinian Jewish Apocalypses." In *Apocalypticism in the Mediterranean World and the Near East*. Proceedings of the International Colloquium on Apocalypticism Uppsala, August 12–17, 1979, edited by David Hellholm, 447–60. Tübingen: J. C .B. Mohr (Paul Siebeck), 1983.

———. *Jesus and Judaism*. Philadelphia: Fortress Press, 1985.

———. *Paul and Palestinian Judaism: A Comparison of Patterns of Religion*. Philadelphia: Fortress Press, 1977.

Schüssler-Fiorenza, Elisabeth. "The Phenomenon of Early Christian Apocalyptic: Some Reflections on Method." In *Apocalypticism in the Mediterranean World and the Near East*. Proceedings of the International Colloquium on Apocalypticism Uppsala, August 12–17, 1979., edited by David Hellholm, 295–316. Tübingen: J. C. B. Mohr (Paul Siebeck), 1983.

———. *The Book of Revelation: Justice and Judgment*. Philadelphia: Fortress Press, 1985.

Schweitzer, Albert. *The Mysticism of Paul the Apostle*. Translated by William B. D. Montgomery, with a preface by Jaroslav Pelikan. 1931. Baltimore: Johns Hopkins University Press, 1998.

———. *The Quest of the Historical Jesus: A Critical Study of Its Progress from Reimarus to Wrede*. Edited by James M. Robinson. Translated by W. B. D. Montgomery. 1968. Baltimore: Johns Hopkins University Press, 1998.

Segal, Paul. *Paul the Convert: The Apostolate and Apostasy of Saul the Pharisee*. New Haven: Yale University Press, 1990.

Sim, D. S. *Apocalyptic Eschatology in the Gospel of Matthew*. Cambridge: Cambridge University Press, 1996.

Sturm, Richard. "Defining the Word 'Apocalyptic': A Problem in Biblical Criticism." In *Apocalyptic and the New Testament: Essays in Honor of J. Louis Martyn,* eds Joel Marcus and Marion Soards, 17–48. Sheffield: JSOT Press, 1989.

Tabor, James D. *Things Unutterable: Paul's Ascent to Paradise in Its Greco-Roman, Judaic, and Early Christian Contexts.* Lanham, Md.: Unversity Press of America, 1986.

Thompson, Leonard. *The Book of Revelation: Apocalypse and Empire.* New York: Oxford University Press, 1990.

————. *Revelation.* Nashville: Abingdon Press, 1998.

Vielhauer, Philip. "Apocalyptic in Early Christianity." Revised by George Strecker. In *New Testament Apocrypha,* edited by William Schneemelcher, translated by R. McL. Wilson. Louisville: Westminster/John Knox Press, 1992, rev. ed.

Watson, Duane F. "Millennium." In *Eerdmans Dictionary of the Bible,* edited by David Noel Freedman, 900–901. Grand Rapids, Mich.: Eerdmans, 2000.

Wink, Walter. *The Powers That Be: Theology for a New Millennium.* New York: Doubleday, 1998.

Wright, N. T. *The New Testament and the People of God.* Minneapolis: Fortress Press, 1992.

————. *Jesus and the Victory of God.* Minneapolis: Fortress Press, 1996.

For Further Reading

Allison, Dale C. "The Eschatology of Jesus." In *The Encyclopedia of Apocalypticism,* edited by John J. Collins, 267–302. New York: Continuum, 1998. Focuses on the eschatology of Jesus from an apocalyptic point of view. This is a condensed version of many of the arguments in his work below.

——. *Jesus of Nazareth. Millenarian Prophet.* Minneapolis: Fortress Press, 1998. Allison defends the view of Jesus as a millenarian or apocalyptic prophet. He critiques rigorously the methodology of Crossan and others. Of special interest is a section on the nature and history of millenarian movements.

Aune, David. *Revelation. Revelation 6–16,* and *Revelation 17–22.* Word Biblical Commentary. Dallas, Tex.: Word Books, 1997, 1998, and 1998 respectively. These three volumes are fine representatives of the historical-critical approach to the study of the Book of Revelation. They are very detailed and complex, so are probably not ideal for entry level readers. They are an excellent tool for a more advanced and detailed study of Revelation in its historical context, as well as the structure and symbolic meaning of the text.

Bauckham, Richard. *The Theology of the Book of Revelation.* Cambridge: Cambridge University Press, 1993. A study of the theology of Revelation and its roots in OT theology and prophecy.

Beale, G. K. *The Book of Revelation.* The New International Greek Testament Commentary. Grand Rapids, Mich.: Eerdmans, 1999. This commentary is daunting in its size, but worth the effort. Eclectic in his approach and evangelical in perspective, Beale opts for what he calls a "redemptive-historical" approach, in that the events prophesied in Revelation are non-particular and recurring in every age of the church's history.

Beker, J. Christiaan. *Paul the Apostle: The Triumph of God in Life and Thought.* Edinburgh: T & T Clark, 1980. Beker's theory of apocalyptic theology as the coherent center of Paul's gospel makes its first appearance in this work. Contains detailed exegetical work; could be tedious for the beginner.

————. *Paul's Apocalyptic Gospel: The Coming Triumph of God.* Philadelphia: Fortress Press, 1982. Beker concentrates on apocalyptic as the essence of Paul's gospel, and as such it cannot be stripped away or attenuated. This is much easier to read than his previous work, and is written with force and passion. A stimulating work; highly recommended.

————. *The Triumph of God: The Essence of Paul's Thought.* Translated by Loren T. Stuckenbruck. Minneapolis: Fortress Press, 1990. This is a later version of his second work. He refines his arguments and responds to criticisms of his previous works.

Borg, Marcus J. In *Jesus in Contemporary Scholarship.* Valley Forge, Pa.: Trinity Press International, 1994. A collection of articles on historical Jesus research, including several of Borg's that argue for a noneschatological Jesus.

Boring, M. Eugene. *Revelation: Interpretation.* Louisville: John Knox Press, 1989. This is a good beginner's commentary, and is oriented toward preaching and teaching. The introductory essay is most helpful, especially its discussion of symbolic language and the various types of interpretation of the Book of Revelation.

Charlesworth, James H., ed. *The Old Testament Pseudepigrapha—Vol. 1: Apocalyptic Literature and Testaments.* New York: Doubleday, 1983. This is the first of a two-volume work. Various Jewish apocalyptic works, such as 1 Enoch, 2 Baruch and 4 Ezra, are translated and analyzed by a team of scholars. Of great interest, and helps to illuminate and contextualize the apocalyptic elements of the New Testament.

Collins, Adela Yarbro. *Crisis and Catharsis:. The Power of the Apocalypse.* Philadelphia: Westminster Press, 1984. An important work that illustrates the possible role of Revelation in a community that was not experiencing persecution. She is especially sensitive to the issue of religious violence and hatred, as well as the uses and abuses of literature such as Revelation.

————. "Apocalypses and Apocalypticism: Early Christian." In *Anchor Bible Dictionary,* 1:288–91. New York: Doubleday, 1992. A useful survey of apocalyptic literature and ideas in early Christianity.

————. "The Influence of Daniel on the New Testament." In *Daniel: A Commentary on the Book of Daniel,* John J. Collins, 90–123. Minneapolis: Fortress Press, 1993. An excellent essay on the influence of Daniel on the New Testament.

Collins, John J., ed. *The Encyclopedia of Apocalypticism.* Vol. 1. New York: Continuum, 1998. The first of a three-volume work, and includes articles by various scholars on the origin, genesis, and development of apocalyptic in the ancient Near East. This volume concludes with discussions of apocalyptic in Paul (de Boer) and the eschatology of Jesus (Allison). Highly recommended.

————. *Daniel: A Commentary on the Book of Daniel.* Hermeneia. Minneapolis: Fortress Press, 1993. A state of the art commentary on the Book of Daniel. In this thorough analysis, Collins covers important topics such as the Son of Man question and the symbolism of chapters 7 and 12. A.Y. Collins includes an essay on the influence of Daniel on the New Testament.

————. *The Apocalyptic Imagination. An Introduction to Jewish Apocalyptic Literature.* Grand Rapids, Mich.: Eerdmans, 1998, rev. ed. The best general introduction to the nature, origin, and development of apocalyptic literature. Collins portrays apocalyptic as a response to periods of struggle and persecution. It serves to form and inspire the religious imagination and to strengthen faith. The concluding chapter discusses the impact of Jewish apocalyptic on the New Testament and the beginnings of Christian apocalyptic.

Crossan, John Dominic. *The Historical Jesus: The Life of a Mediterranean Jewish Peasant.* San Francisco: HarperSanFrancisco, 1991. This controversial and challenging work set the agenda for much of the historical Jesus research of the 1990s. Crossan writes in a very eloquent and appealing style, and his portrayals of the political and social milieu of first-century Palestine are especially vivid and detailed. Crossan's reconstruction of Jesus is very different from the conventional one. Jesus is a peasant revolutionary and is a product of his social, political, and economic environment. Crossan's methodology is carefully explained.

———. *Jesus: A Revolutionary Biography.* San Francisco: HarperSanFrancisco, 1994. This is a short popular version of his previous work. Very user-friendly, but does not lose any of the essence of his arguments.

de Boer, Martinus C. "Paul and Apocalyptic Eschatology." In *The Encyclopedia of Apocalyptic,* edited by John J. Collins, 345–83. New York: Continuum, 1998. A summary and updating of his two previous works. He covers a number of issues: the forensic and cosmological streams of apocalyptic, Paul's apocalyptic reinterpretation of death, and whether Paul's theology of salvation was universal.

Decock, Paul B. "Some Issues in Apocalyptic in the Exegetical Literature of the Last Ten Years." *Neotestamentica* 33, no. 1 (1999): 1–31. Decock discusses some of the currents in apocalyptic research of the past few years, especially the ongoing debate concerning the definition of the apocalyptic genre. Good for a broad general view of recent research.

Duff, Paul. "Reading the Apocalypse at the Millennium." *Religious Studies Review* 26, no. 3 (July 2000): 217–22. Duff surveys a few of the recent commentaries on the Book of Revelation with brief comments on the strengths and weaknesses of each.

Ehrman, Bart D. *Jesus: Apocalyptic Prophet of the New Millennium.* Minneapolis: Fortress Press, 1999. One of several books that Ehrman has written for general readers. He explains the fundamentals of NT scholarship as he builds a solid case for Jesus the apocalyptic prophet. Ehrman writes in an enjoyable and humorous style that is jargon free and accessible to all. Highly recommended.

Fredriksen, Paula. *Jesus of Nazareth: King of the Jews.* New York: Vintage Books, 1999. Fredriksen is especially successful in portraying Jesus in his Jewish milieu. Her evocative portrayal of the formative influences on Jesus is interesting. She argues for the apocalyptic nature of his preaching and ministry. She is in the tradition of E. P. Sanders but disagrees with him on a few key points.

Hanson, Paul. "Apocalypses and Apocalypticism." In *Anchor Bible Dictionary,* 1:279–82. New York: Doubleday, 1992. A condensed but useful survey of the topic. Hanson's views concerning the origins of apocalyptic theology are highlighted.

Hellholm, D., ed. *Apocalypticism in the Mediterranean World and the Near East.* Proceedings of the International Colloquium on Apocalypticism, Uppsala, August 12–17, 1979. Tübingen: Mohr (Siebeck), 1983. Contains papers in French, German, and English given at an international conference on apocalypticism. The papers cover a wide variety of topics and represent the best in international scholarship. Useful for those desiring more detailed and technical information.

Jacobsen, David Schnasa. *Preaching in the New Creation.* Louisville, Ky.: Westminster John Knox Press, 1999. Jacobsen confronts the difficulty of preaching on apocalyptic texts. He offers a sound method and includes several sample homilies on various passages.

Kloppenborg Verbin, John S. *Excavating Q: The History and Settings of the Sayings Gospel.* Edinburgh: T & T Clark, 2000. Kloppenborg is one of the foremost scholars in Q research. This books represents the last two decades of his work in this area, and features a good history of the problem with a detailed analysis of this controversial source.

Martyn, J. Louis. *Theological Issues in the Letters of Paul.* Nashville: Abingdon Press, 1997. A collection of Martyn's articles concentrating on the letters of Paul. Contains the four important articles on apocalyptic discussed in chapter 3.

McGinn, Bernard, ed. *The Encyclopedia of Apocalypticism.* Vol. 2. New York: Continuum, 1998. The second of three volumes. Articles by several scholars trace apocalyptic theology, spirituality, and religious movements from the period of the early church to the early modern period. Highly recommended.

Reddish, Mitchell G. *Apocalyptic Literature: A Reader.* Peabody, Mass.: Hendrickson, 1995. A collection of selected passages of various Jewish and Christian apocalyptic works of the NT period. Short but helpful introductions are included. This is an excellent book for introductory courses and Bible study groups.

Richard, Pablo. *Apocalypse: A People's Commentary on the Book of Revelation.* Maryknoll, N.Y.: Orbis Books, 1995. A relentlessly liberationist interpretation of Revelation. He takes the historical context seriously, but seeks to anchor it firmly in our contemporary world. Very thought-provoking and a good counterbalance to some of the more extreme spiritualizing tendencies of our day.

Russell, D. S. *Divine Disclosure: An Introduction to Jewish Apocalyptic.* London, 1992. A brief and readable but reliable survey of Jewish apocalyptic. This is a summary and refinement of his *Method and Message of Jewish Apocalyptic,* which was written nearly thirty years before.

Sanders, E. P. *Jesus and Judaism.* Philadelphia: Fortress Press, 1985. Jesus is seen as part of the experience of Second Temple Judaism. His ministry and message reflect the apocalyptic expectations of this period, and point to the renewal and restoration of Israel.

Schüssler-Fiorenza, Elisabeth. *The Book of Revelation: Justice and Judgment.* Philadelphia: Fortress Press, 1985; *The Book of Revelation: Justice and Thought.* Minneapolis: Fortress Press, 1999. The latter book is a new edition. Schüssler-Fiorenza's work is a fine example of rhetorical analysis. She takes very seriously the justice component of Revelation and shows how apocalyptic was a vital element in early Christian communities.

Stein, Stephen J., ed. *The Encyclopedia of Apocalypticism.* Vol. 3. New York: Continuum, 1998. This volume covers apocalypticism as a social and religious phenomenon in the modern period and the contemporary age.

Thompson, Leonard. *The Book of Revelation: Apocalypse and Empire.* New York: Oxford University Press, 1990. Thompson's historical-critical study of Revelation and its background challenges the received wisdom that the intended audience of the Revelation was experiencing persecution.

————. *Revelation.* Nashville: Abingdon Press, 1998. This is a commentary that condenses much of the information from his earlier research. Good for introductory courses.

Watson, Duane F. "Millennium." In *Eerdmans Dictionary of the Bible,* edited by David Noel Freedman, 900–901. Grand Rapids, Mich.: Eerdmans, 2000. A good description of the different sorts of apocalyptic worldviews, such as "millennial" and "premillennial."

Weber, Eugene. *Apocalypses. Prophecies, Cults and Millennial Beliefs through the Ages.* Cambridge: Harvard University Press, 1999. A brief and fascinating history of apocalyptic and millennial movements throughout history. This book helps to put many of the current millennial claims in historical perspective. Highly recommended.

Wink, Walter. *The Powers That Be: Theology for a New Millennium.* New York: Doubleday, 1998. A challenging and inspiring appropriation of some of the New Testament's apocalyptic symbolism, especially the language of spiritual struggle with unseen powers.

The spirituality of social justice, nonviolence, and reconciliation is its modern expression. Highly recommended.

Wright, N. T. *Jesus and the Victory of God.* Minneapolis: Fortress, 1996. This is the second volume of his series, following *The New Testament and the People of God.* Wright portrays Jesus as an apocalyptic messenger, but insists that apocalyptic language in the New Testament was not intended to be literal in its depiction of the end of the world. He critiques the methodology and reconstructions of Crossan and the Jesus Seminar.

————. *The Millennium Myth: Hope for a Postmodern World.* Louisville: Westminster John Knox Press, 1999. Wright focuses on the "millennial fever" of the last few years and shows how much of it is based on misconceptions of apocalyptic theology and literature. We are not facing the end of the world, but a challenge to our social and cultural symbols. Apocalyptic hope can heal much of the malaise of our time. Wright shows how to take the new millennium and the apocalyptic message seriously but not literally.

Other Books in This Series